CHILDREN OF THE RICH

CHILDREN OF THE RICH

BURTON N. WIXEN, M.D.

CROWN PUBLISHERS, INC., NEW YORK

© 1973 by Burton N. Wixen

All rights reserved. No part of this book may be reproduced or utilized in any form or by any means, electronic or mechanical, including photocopying, recording, or by any information storage and retrieval system, without permission in writing from the Publisher. Inquiries should be addressed to Crown Publishers, Inc., 419 Park Avenue South, New York, N.Y. 10016

Library of Congress Catalog Card Number: 72-96646
ISBN: 0-517-503603

Printed in the United States of America

Published simultaneously in Canada by General Publishing Company Limited

Designed by Ruth Smerechniak

TO ADELA ROGERS ST. JOHNS, WHO ENCOURAGED ME TO WRITE THIS BOOK, WITH LOVE AND APPRECIATION

For unto whomsoever much is given, of him shall be much required: and to whom men have committed much, of him they will ask the more.

LUKE 12:48

For of those to whom much is given, much is required.

JOHN FITZGERALD KENNEDY
Inaugural Address
January 20, 1961

CONTENTS

1 A WASTED RESOURCE 3
2 BREWER 5
3 BREWER'S THERAPY 14
4 NEUROSIS AND IDENTITY PROBLEMS 24
5 DYSGRADIA 35
6 WILSON 44

7	PAMELA	52
8	AN OVERVIEW	61
9	JUNE	66
10	CHILDREN OF THE POOR	75
11	THE GOLDEN GHETTO	83
12	YOU CAN'T SAY NO TO ME! The Story of Cleo	87
13	SELF-TREATMENT	104
14	THE ANALYTICAL APPROACH TO TREATMENT	112
15	IVAN: THE CRISIS	117
16	IVAN: ATTACKING DYSGRADIA	124
17	IVAN: THE ANALYSIS	131
18	COUNTERTRANSFERENCE	141
19	A SUITE AT THE TOP WITH INSURANCE	149
20	THE GRAND ALLIANCE OF RICH AND POOR	154
21	CORS ANONYMOUS	159
22	THE SUCCESSFUL RICH	164
23	PREVENTION	170
24	NEUROSES OF MOBILITY	176
25	JOHN	183
26	NEW LIFE-STYLES	201
27	CONCLUSION	206

CHILDREN OF THE RICH

1

A WASTED RESOURCE

THIS BOOK IS ABOUT PEOPLE WITH GREAT POTENTIAL who are leading meaningless lives. They are very wealthy, but their wealth gives them very little pleasure. On the contrary, the life-styles made possible by their affluence have turned out to be traps from which too few manage to escape. Many could be creative and productive. They and their wealth are a wasted resource for our country.

In spite of unforgivable bigotry and injustice, our country has the most mobile class structure the world has ever known. As great numbers of people move upward in their social status, they encounter problems in themselves and their children that they are unprepared for. They find themselves at crossroads which represent crucial stages for the future history of their families. A failure to recognize what is happening as life-styles begin to change may sentence an entire family to dead-end lives.

As a psychiatrist and psychoanalyst, I have known and tried to help some of these disadvantaged rich. I have also worked with many people caught in crises produced by rapid changes in their social positions. Usually it is the children and young adults who suffer the most and for whom the most can be done. Some of their stories will be told to illustrate particular aspects of these problems.

In describing case histories one runs into a serious problem. Anyone entering therapy is assured complete and total confidentiality. This trust must be inviolable for any type of therapy to proceed. And yet it is important to draw attention to this unlikely group of underprivileged. The only solution to this dilemma is to fictionalize their stories totally. The names, locales, schools, family constellations, and all other details are completely fabricated. However, the psychological truth is precisely preserved.

2

BREWER

I REMEMBER LOS ANGELES IN THE MID-THIRTIES. MAYBE the exuberance of youth colored my perceptions, but I clearly remember seeing the purple mountains to the north every day. In the winter they were snowcapped, though I was well into my teens before I journeyed past the orange groves up those mountains to actually feel snow on my face. On Saturday night I would travel downtown with my family on the number seven streetcar to attend the old Million-Dollar Theatre. A few years later it was the Orpheum—ten acts of vaudeville, two features, and a keno game which presented a new Chevrolet to the lucky winner. Los Angeles's romance with the automobile was just beginning. That's where Brewer's family came in.

Grandfather Clarke had been a mechanic in Toledo. He'd started working in a carriage shop, but quickly became fascinated with the internal-combustion engine. Nobody knows why he left for Los Angeles in the early thirties. One day he announced to his wife they were going. They took their modest possessions in a well-cared-for Model T, along with their two teenage sons and headed west.

Was it sheer good fortune or was it an uncanny sense of what the future held? Los Angeles was a medium-size city with small clusters of settlements (metastases?) reaching in all directions. The transportation system consisted of slow, rumbling yellow streetcars within the city, and big red interurban streetcars reaching beyond. They were slow and infrequent, but there weren't very many people going anywhere. Grandpa Clarke was a taciturn man, and in later years when he was interviewed he didn't have much to say. For some reason he staked his future on the automobile with remarkable success.

Grandpa Clarke went to work as a mechanic. He was good at his trade, and thrift was a strong point with him. He accumulated a fair nest egg and bought a small garage of his own just outside the city. When the war came he kept the garage open and took a swing-shift job at an aircraft company. His family didn't understand why he insisted on buying up open fields of land behind his garage, but by the time the war ended he owned considerable frontage on both sides of his garage, and a total of five acres of land in back.

When Grandpa Clarke's two sons returned home from the army in 1946, Philip was twenty-six and Mark was twenty-eight. Since childhood they had helped around their father's garage, and after special schooling in the army they served their country as truck mechanics. The three of them worked well together in the family garage, although as business grew Mark attended more and more to the business end of things. He persuaded his father and brother to invest in an automobile franchise which began to flourish immediately. Mark quickly grasped the potential of television, and soon Clarke Motors was being promoted nightly on wrestling matches and old cowboy movies.

Los Angeles began to burst its seams. Ribbons of concrete freeways spread in all directions. One passed directly by Clarke Motors. Soon it was in the center of tremendous population growth and was one of the largest dealerships in the country. The empty fields around the garage were flag-covered car lots, showrooms, and service facilities. By then Los Angeles was the most car-glutted city on earth. Smog choked the basin; the mountains were no longer visible to the north; and the Clarkes were millionaires.

Grandpa Clarke changed very little: he was tall, thin, tanned, with silver hair setting off his deeply creased face. He could have passed for a ranch hand on one of the late, late shows. He expanded the business, invested in a TV station, and bought land. He and his wife lived in a $50,000 house within a mile of Clarke Motors. He went to work each day and supervised the service department until he died quite suddenly at seventy-three. His wife lived on a few more years but turned things completely over to her sons.

Mark resembled his father, but was not quite as rugged

looking. He was not in the sun much and tended to be somewhat heavy. He and his brother had ended their formal education when they entered the army after high school, but Mark had the wisdom to hire topflight business managers and to learn from them. He gradually went into work less and less, until finally he attended a meeting one morning a week. Philip had no great interest in the business and was very happy to collect his dividends and let Mark run things.

Philip moved to the colony at Malibu where he drank heavily, gave sumptuous parties, and boasted that he never slept with the same girl twice. He was found one morning drowned in his own vomitus. Several women turned up claiming to be mothers of Philip's children. After several very well publicized court trials, the entire estate went to Mark.

Mark was worth at least $5,000,000 and probably a great deal more. The businesses ran themselves and Mark continued to attend only one weekly meeting with his lieutenants. He took a suite at the Bel Air Hotel and became a popular man-about-town. His name was often in the society columns and his affairs were with well-known Californians. Portia Handley was his most frequent date. Her family's wealth was from old eastern industry and West Coast oil, and the idea of "old money" and "old families" appealed to him. She was a tall, blond, blue-eyed beauty who longed for love but was afraid of any real intimacy. She welcomed Mark's ardent lovemaking at first, but as she felt his affection growing she became more and more frightened and finally completely frigid. Mark was not particularly perceptive about what was happening, and when Portia became pregnant they decided to marry.

There was not much love in this marriage. Mark liked her looks and her family position. She had to marry to protect her family. It was a huge wedding, attended by the governor. They traveled around the world on their honeymoon, though Portia had too much morning sickness to be a very ardent lover, at least that was her most common excuse. By the time they returned to Los Angeles, Mark knew he had erred, but was determined to make the best of it. A famous architect was called in to design their home. It would have five hilltop acres in Bel Air with a breathtaking view of the city below—when the latter was not blotted out by an acrid, yellow haze of poisonous fumes. Mark used to joke that between the automobiles Clarke Motors had sold, and the gas and oil that Handley Industries pumped, refined, and marketed, their families accounted for one-fourteenth of all Los Angeles air pollution.

Out of this unhappy union was born Brewer Philip Clarke. His father was proud and prophesied that this child would someday be responsible for a full one-eighth of his city's pollution. His mother became severely depressed and went to bed. The home was completed and was magnificent; they named it Clarkeview. Portia showed little interest in her baby but the child was by no means neglected. Three shifts of RNs attended the infant for a year. The house staff consisted of maids, cooks, and chauffeurs. Portia would visit Brewer each day when she felt up to it. She was diagnosed as suffering from a postpartum depression by their family physician and was referred to a psychiatrist. She apparently was unwilling to explore her unhappy marriage and frigidity and soon broke off treatment. She began drinking heavily and visited her son only rarely. When Mark found her in bed with the Cuban cook, she agreed to leave and give custody of Brewer to Mark.

After Brewer was two his care was entrusted to Elsie, a large, warm black woman of around fifty. Her entire life revolved around her ward, and she seldom bothered to take her days off. She read to him, hugged him, played with him, went for rides with him, and ate with him. Father had resumed his social life after the divorce and rarely dined at home. When Brewer was five, he was started in a private school. On special occasions he would dine with his father and perhaps a few guests.

Mark sincerely loved Brewer. He felt a tenderness and warmth for the child that were very genuine. Brewer was bright and handsome and, though he resembled his father, had his mother's blue eyes and blond hair. He was naturally athletic. Almost every day before breakfast Mark would walk with the boy around the grounds of Clarkeview. They would wrestle, play with the dogs, swim, or talk about automobiles. Brewer loved his father, but he feared him too. Mark had become used to giving orders and expected complete obedience from Brewer. He strapped Brewer when he was recalcitrant, which was seldom. After the morning playtime, he was given back over to Elsie as Father's sports car or limousine pulled away.

On school vacations Brewer would go down to Clarke Motors with his father for the weekly staff meeting. This was a very special day. The ride in the limousine was thrilling, watching people in nearby cars craning to see what famous person was out riding. The respect that Father commanded was awesome: "Good morning, Mr. Clarke"; "Good morning, sir"; and a very special kind of look from his private secretary—who had to be the most beautiful woman in the world.

At the meeting ice water, coffee, cigarettes were supplied his father, while he was provided with hot chocolate and cookies. Complicated business proposals were presented to his father who would then make a binding pronouncement. It was marvelous! What power his father possessed! What wisdom! "And someday I'll be sitting in that chair!" His father was actually by then rather plump and pale and had become arrogant in his dealings with his staff. Brewer mistook their fear and obsequiousness for homage to a great man, but it was great stuff to glory in. After the meeting Mark and Brewer would walk through the showrooms and service facilities; more showers of respect and attention. When they were home Brewer would tell Elsie all about it, and she would echo his expectations, "Mistah Brewer, someday you'll tell them how to run the whole business. Won't that be sumthin'!"

Brewer did well in school. He was popular and had an easy, confident manner. He received As and Bs with minimal effort. He was an outstanding athlete and starred in basketball and tennis. When he was fourteen, a shapely red-haired Irish maid of twenty-five came into his bed one night and taught him to make love. She came almost every night from then on; his grades went down only a little and he dropped basketball. By the time she returned to Ireland three years later, Brewer had a harem of girl friends to sleep with.

Brewer was accepted by Stanford, the only college he applied to. A large party sent him off. His father arranged to have his bank deposit $1,000 a month to Brewer's account, in addition to paying tuition and the upkeep on his Porsche. Trouble began immediately. Brewer was involved in accident after accident, until he became an assigned insurance risk. He forced another car off the road, causing the driver to lose an eye. He would sleep much of the day and drive his Porsche at high speeds around back roads for much of the night. He was failing in his classes and, after the first quarter, was on probation. He smoked a lot of marijuana, drank excessively, and began getting heavy. He contracted gonorrhea twice and had to pay for a girl's abortion. His father was becoming angry.

Brewer had great difficulty managing money. He would often spend most of his month's allowance in a week or so and then borrow money from friends or write bad checks for the remainder of the month. His bank would usually pass the checks and his father would cover them. The expenditures were usually frivolous: cases of fine French wines in the closets of his apartment; flights to Las Vegas for an evening with ten or twelve friends as his guests; telephone calls to acquaintances all over the world; a round trip ticket for a casual girl friend to visit her family in New York. Sometimes he would finish out a month living on bread and grape jelly.

His father visited him every few weeks and they would have long conversations. At first Mark attempted to work out budgets for him, and Brewer would dutifully study them, make suggestions, and then solemnly resolve to follow them. His efforts seldom lasted more than a few days. His father would return for the next crisis and threaten to cut off all Brewer's income unless things improved. Brewer was always reasonable. He always admitted his errors, was contrite while his father scolded, and absolutely sincere in his resolutions.

Father consulted a psychologist in Palo Alto. He met with

Brewer, then Father, then the two together. As always Brewer was completely reasonable and agreed that he must accept certain responsibilities in return for his father's support. If he could not bring his grades up to passing, he would not receive his college allowance and would have to return home. He could have tutors and all the help he needed. He would turn the Porsche over to his father for thirty days. After that he could keep it only so long as his driving record was satisfactory. In the meantime he would bicycle to class. He was getting heavy and the exercise would do him good. He would see the psychologist twice a week and would receive his allowance in weekly payments.

Brewer faithfully kept the appointments with his doctor, but did nothing else. He was amiable and earnest in discussing his problems, he would go over and over the ways he had misused his money. He would resolve to study for an exam and then frankly describe how he went out and got drunk instead. He and his doctor explored the effect this was having on his life and on his relationship with his father. They concluded that he was acting out anger at his father in a most self-destructive manner. A dream suggested to them that Brewer blamed his father for sending Mother away. Nothing changed and Brewer was dropped from school. His allowance was stopped and he returned home to Clarkeview.

He and his father barely spoke for weeks. Brewer would sleep a great deal of the day and spend the evening with friends. He was close to losing his driver's license and so restrained his driving. He found plenty of "action" with his friends and seemed to get along well without much money. His father suggested he enter psychotherapy and Brewer agreed. That's how I met him.

3

BREWER'S THERAPY

BREWER WAS EIGHTEEN. HE WAS IV-F BECAUSE OF FLAT feet. He was about five feet ten and weighed almost 230 pounds. He was handsome and resembled his father, whom I remembered seeing years before, selling cars on television. The blond hair he'd had as a child was now light brown, and his eyes a very pale blue. He was confident, poised, intelligent, and perceptive. He asked how we should begin, and I asked him what he wanted me to help him with. He described himself as very happy and stable until he went away to college when "everything crashed." He carefully described his problems with money, his driving, and schoolwork. When I asked why he thought things had "crashed," he replied, "I was—and am—simply too immature to cope with the responsibility. I don't know how much I was trying to spite my father, but that's some of it. I just need to grow up. I guess I've been spoiled rotten." He sounded sincere, though superficial, and I felt we could work together.

I'll describe my initial thinking as accurately as I can recall it. I weighed the possibility that he suffered from an impulse neurosis or some such form of character disorder. Such patients are very difficult—sometimes impossible—to treat because they can tolerate so little anxiety. The least bit of tension is immediately converted into some poorly thought-out impulsive action. The ability to bear anxiety and analyze its causes during the therapy hours is virtually absent. I hoped this would not prove to be the case because it carried such a grave prognosis for treatment, but it was compatible with the aimless impulsiveness of his past year and in keeping with his likable superficiality and apparent freedom from anxiety. Against that diagnosis was his long history of excellent performance in all his undertakings prior to college. In addition, since leaving college his chaotic life-style had settled down considerably.

I considered the possibility of an underlying depression stimulated by leaving home alone for virtually the first time in his life. (He had traveled extensively around the world, but always with his father and Elsie.) There was some memory of a depression at summer camp when he was nine, and he never went again. Perhaps leaving his father, friends, and Elsie when he went to college produced a depression that he warded off by his frantic racing behavior.

There was the possibility, raised in his brief period of therapy at Stanford, that the increased personal freedom he felt at college allowed a long dormant hostility toward his father to surface; this was expressed in the innumerable ways he frustrated his father and in his guilty need for punishment satisfied by his self-destructiveness.

While one inevitably considers various possible sets of dynamics in undertaking psychotherapy, fortunately it is not necessary, and as a matter of fact is undesirable, to have it all worked out from the onset. Any course of therapy is filled with surprises, and these initial thoughts by no means exhausted the possibilities. One need only decide whether the probabilities are favorable for an insight-oriented type of therapy to proceed and then be prepared to learn with the patient. I liked Brewer, felt he was bright, perceptive, and well motivated. His father was quite sophisticated about the "ground rules" of analysis and realized his need to stay out of it and leave it entirely between Brewer and me. It was decided Brewer would pay my fee himself from a trust fund his grandfather had left him.

I was aware that I was pleased to have Brewer as a patient. His family name was well known in this area. He could pay a good fee, though I purposely did not go above the upper range of my usual fees. I felt some pride that this prominent family had selected me. In brief, I felt my countertransference feelings were conscious and would not represent an impediment to treatment. My decision initially was to use conventional psychoanalysis as the treatment of choice. I was later to find that in treating such patients there are times when considerable flexibility is called for.

We got off to a good start. I saw him five times a week, utilizing the couch, free association, dream, and transference analysis. The first dream in an analysis is often very significant. This was Brewer's: He visits his father at the old garage his grandfather had started. A mechanic is teaching him something about repairing cars. He slides underneath a car and awakens with a fright when hot grease splashes on his face and eyes.

The understanding of a dream is derived by following the free associations to each bit of it. There is always more to each dream than can be fruitfully analyzed; references to past memories, current life conflicts, and the relationship with the analyst are present. These were Brewer's associations: (1) Visiting his father at grandfather's old garage: Fond memories of a very happy childhood connected closely with the family business; those exciting meetings he would attend with Father; rides the mechanics would give him when they test-drove cars—he'd often spend school holidays and summer vacations hanging around the garage; his uncertainty about the future—he had always assumed he would follow his father into the business, but now father seemed doubtful about his dependability; he "ran out" of further associations as a hint of hostility toward his father emerged —repression set in as his anxiety warned him he was entering dangerous territory. (2) A mechanic is teaching him: He wished he knew more about the business; shame about failing in school; an appreciative feeling toward the mechanic makes him think of positive feelings he is beginning to have toward me; the position under the car associates to the couch. (3) Hot grease splashes his face and eyes: Nothing occurs to him.

The first train of associations breaks off with a hint of hostility toward Father. The second ends with thoughts of affectionate feelings toward me and lying on the couch. My formulation (to myself) was that the injury to his face and eyes represented the unconscious fear of castration, the fear of horrible, mutilating punishment for hostile feelings toward Father. Probably his developing affectionate feelings toward me and the passive position on the couch were also felt as a danger. What part of all this should I comment on? The developing positive transference isn't threatening enough to need an interpretation at this point. The conflict with Father is too far from the surface. One must start from the surface and later move to deeper levels. I choose to comment on his foremost present concern, "The dream indicates anxiety about what you are going to do in life." He agrees and expands in considerable detail about his present uncertainties.

An analysis never proceeds in a straight line or at an even pace. There is progression, regression, resistance; periods during which meaningful insight is gained are followed by weeks of apparent stalemate. In many ways, Brewer's analysis progressed in as close to a "typical manner" as one ever encounters. My feeling that impulsivity was not the primary way he dealt with anxiety was borne out. He kept his appointments faithfully even when he was sick, paid his bill promptly, was never late. The importance to him of the family business and the family name came up again and again.

Brewer was proud of the Clarke name. He glowed when

people asked: "Clarke of Clarke Motors?" He admitted pleasure in knowing that he was sole heir to the family business. His father's warm, affectionate relationship with him had soured considerably during the period at Stanford. Now as Brewer worked seriously in his analysis, kept decent hours, seemed to be driving carefully, and even doing some gardening around the house, Mark began to regain his old trust for Brewer. They had some conversations about his coming to work for the dealership; Brewer was enthusiastic.

When he discussed the question of going to work for Clarke Motors in his analysis, I was strictly neutral. We analyzed his feelings connected with it—ambivalence toward Father, fantasies of Father's dying and his becoming president, a fear that latent problems between them might become open. Mark felt Brewer had to earn the respect of the business staff, he didn't want them to feel the boss's son was being pushed on them. He wanted Brewer to start in the shop as a mechanic's helper for maybe six months, then spend some time on the used car lot, then new car sales, finally working into the broader aspects of the business—advertising, financing, the nonautomotive investments. He foresaw a three- or four-year program to prepare Brewer for a major managerial position. This program seemed very reasonable to Brewer; he was eager to begin.

The job at Clarke Motors was a disaster. I was frankly surprised. Brewer seemed so serious and well motivated that I was not prepared for what happened. He arrived two hours late his first day on the job and, while filling out the employment forms, made a pass at the personnel clerk, who turned out to be pregnant and married to the service manager. Father had an excellent intelligence network and knew of these events by lunchtime. He picked Brewer up at the garage for lunch and gave him hell. Brewer was contrite. When he came for his hour with me at five thirty he wept. "I don't know what got into me! I just wasn't thinking. I didn't want to embarrass Dad—or did I?"

We explored the obvious inappropriateness of his behavior and concluded that he was indeed acting out hostility toward his father in a very self-destructive way. I believe that formulation was true, but was only part of the story.

He remained on the job, but inappropriateness in his behavior continued. In his dealings with me he never seemed bizarre in any way. Yet at work he was constantly in trouble. He'd pinch a secretary's bottom; he was chronically late; he entertained the mechanics with witty stories until they complained that they couldn't do their work. His behavior was clearly self-destructive. Did he feel guilt about his death wishes toward Father? Did he need to embarrass him even at the expense of his own reputation? Was he fooling me by convincing me of his earnestness? We went over and over all of this.

Brewer was fired by his father after two weeks. I felt I had done my best to confront him with the direction he was heading into and to explore the possible motives. I was disappointed when he was fired. Was that his motivation? What was most puzzling was that he appeared to work seriously in his analysis and yet the downhill course progressed without being deterred. Often a psychiatrist can head off such acute episodes of self-destructive acting-out. Brewer did not appear to be a chronically self-defeating character. "Acting-out" implies a turning into real-life action certain impulses and feelings mobilized in the analysis, to avoid analyzing them. In retrospect I'm not sure this would completely fit Brewer's work experience at Clarke Motors.

After he left the job, he was moderately depressed for several weeks and then resumed the relaxed, aimless style of life he had had before. After Father cooled off for a few weeks, he and Brewer would dine together, travel a little on brief vacations, and in general got along very well. Father was frank in discussing his disappointment with Brewer's work performance, but would half-kiddingly state, "Anyway, thank God you have your grandfather's trust fund, and I'll leave you a well-administered trust, so you'll never be on state aid." I asked myself, "Does Mark have a need for Brewer to be a failure? Is Brewer complying with his father's wish?" I'm not sure Brewer or his father saw him as such a failure. My own values about work and advancement were coming into play here.

My background had been thoroughly middle-class. To work hard, get a useful education, apply that education to some endeavor that would advance me socioeconomically—those values had been instilled in me since I was in the crib. They did not necessarily have any meaning for Brewer. He had no need to go anywhere socioeconomically. What then seemed like failure to me had no similar meaning to him. Mark had had a sufficiently middle-class background to share many of my values, and he had genuinely hoped that Brewer would follow him in the business. However, he understood better than I that Brewer was not a failure, that the old values no longer had a practical meaning for him.

Well, what happened to Brewer? We worked together for two and a half years. It was a successful analysis in that the basic neurotic problems were resolved. In addition to his conflicts with Father, it became apparent that he had serious difficulties in his relationships with women. He had learned the story of Mother's inadequacy when he was quite young and harbored a deep distrust of all women. He tended to seek older, motherly women—Elsie was the only woman he had ever come close to trusting. His relationships with girls his age and younger usually lasted one night.

Throughout the analysis he was unable to hold a job for more than a month or two. He loved music and thought he might like to open a hi-fi equipment store. He took a job in such an establishment to learn something about it and was fired in a week. There was never any real need for him to work. He had all the money he would ever need to live on, and my promise that his keeping a job would enable us to work on certain problem areas did not impress him much. The problem concerning work was something different from the usual neurotic conflicts I was prepared to deal with. Only later did I begin to understand what it meant.

He finally decided to move away from Clarkeview. That was not an easy step for him; there he had complete privacy when he wished, a staff of servants to wait on him, and virtually any comfort he could desire. He took a moderately expensive apartment on Wilshire Boulevard and began living with Claire, a student at UCLA. She was from Philadelphia and from a wealthy family. She was attractive and intelligent, and he adored her. The relationship lasted throughout the last year of his analysis, and he seemed truly able to give and receive love from her.

He and I both began to think of terminating his analysis at around the same time. He was maintaining a stable relationship with Claire and was auditing a number of business courses at UCLA. He didn't have a job, but by then I had begun to develop a different outlook on that subject; I felt certain he would eventually commit himself to some worthwhile pursuit. I had tried very diligently to keep my personal values out of the analysis, and, indeed, he did not have very much of my "social conscience." The termination went smoothly.

A few months later I received an announcement of his wedding to Claire in Philadelphia. He had taken over the management of one of her father's hotels in New York. Since then I've heard from him a few times—a birth announcement, occasional short letters. Nothing earthshaking, but he's able to love a woman, work smoothly with men, and gain satisfaction in the business world. His last note described a boys' club he had become interested in; perhaps some social conscience is stirring within him.

I'll always be grateful to Brewer for what he taught me. He had certain more or less typical neurotic problems that I was quite used to dealing with. But there was something else also present, a defect in his personality more directly related to the social changes which had taken place in his family. A few final comments on Brewer must await a discussion of what is meant by "typical neurotic problems," and how emotional problems are influenced by society and social change.

4

NEUROSIS AND IDENTITY PROBLEMS

THE GREATEST DISCOVERY OF SIGMUND FREUD WAS THAT neurosis was the result of unconscious conflict. An impulse or drive comes into conflict with a disapproving part of the mind called the superego (which includes the concept of conscience), and some form of symptomatology results from this internal struggle. For many years, patients with such conflict neuroses represented the majority of cases seen by

NEUROSIS AND IDENTITY PROBLEMS

analysts. The conflicts usually centered around sexual and aggressive drives and resulted in symptoms and internal suffering without any major disruption in functioning.

An example of a typical neurosis involving a sexual conflict is adolescent guilt about masturbation. There, a strong upsurge of sexual drive is countered by a strong conscience which says, "Don't touch yourself! It's dirty and bad and you might injure yourself." The suffering boy goes through agonies of self-hate. The symptom that results might be a hand-washing compulsion, revealing the underlying conflict only to a trained observer. The treatment involves, basically, tracing the symptom back to the conflict and resolving the guilt.

A typical neurosis involving conflict about aggression involves work inhibitions. A businessman might consult a psychiatrist because he becomes anxious whenever he must deal with his boss. His career is in jeopardy and, of course, his self-esteem has plummeted. Analysis reveals a conflict between aggressiveness at work and a disapproving conscience. He unconsciously equates aggressiveness and healthy self-assertion with a naughty child being hostile and defiant to his father. The anxiety with his boss involves guilt about long-forgotten anger toward his father. The treatment involves analyzing these unconscious meanings and resolving the guilt. (As with the previous example, easier said than done.)

It is now recognized that certain conflict neuroses become incorporated into a particular life-style that hides the underlying conflict. An example would be a hostile, angry man who avoids conflict with his conscience by assuming an extremely passive personality. He avoids anxiety by avoiding any aggressive activity, and yet he expresses his hostility by constantly frustrating those who would depend on him. Such situations are called character neuroses. In therapy, the underlying conflict areas become clear as the behavioral patterns are given up.

These neuroses imply a fairly healthy basic personality. The superego may be too strict and its demands very difficult to live up to, but there is a basic sense of where the individual is in society and the roles he aspires to. The businessman wants to progress in his work and achieve certain goals; the adolescent with the hand-washing compulsion is still concerned with doing well in school and following a career path. These problems are the result of internal conflict, though the roots go back to relationships within the family. The effect of changes in society and one's position in society are relatively unimportant.

In recent years, psychiatrists have been confronted increasingly with problems that do not represent classical conflict neuroses nor character neuroses, and in which the role of society is of more immediate importance. These problems are more directly related to conflicts between the individual's cultural heritage and the actual social situation he finds himself in. The more recent recognition of these problems is partly due to a broadening perspective on the part of psychiatrists, but of greater importance are the tremendous social changes that have made these problems much more common. The great psychoanalyst Erik Erikson has focused attention on these problems under the general concept of "identity." An understanding of the concept of identity, and of the stages of development that ultimately result in a sense of identity, is essential to an understanding of these problems.

In the average environment there is a series of developmental stages, under the influence of biological and social forces, that the child passes through. Each stage has its own developmental tasks to accomplish. The concept of these stages adds the influence of society to the foundation of basic psychoanalytic theory with its focus on instinctual drives and conflicts concerning them. As the individual progresses through these stages, he also passes through a whole series of parallel *roles*. The earliest roles are more or less biologically determined. He is an infant at the breast, then a child crawling through the house attempting to put everything in his mouth, then a toddler. Beyond that, society's influence becomes of ever greater importance for each succeeding role situation; he must be helped to develop a mental image of what he can expect to become next. These mental images of what the child can expect to become, and what he is expected to become, might be called *role preimages*.

The toddler gets a hint that he will soon be going off to nursery school. Before he finds himself in that situation, he develops a set of images—many of them possibly inaccurate—of what he will be like at that time. He must go off at regular intervals to a place where he is told he will play and have fun. While his role preimage of himself as a nursery school child is rudimentary, it is of tremendous importance in limiting the anxiety of a major new experience. The more accurate the role image is, the less anxiety, and with each successive level of development, the role preimages are likely to be more accurate.

Ordinarily the child approaching kindergarten has a pretty good idea of what he will be like when he actually steps into that role. The role preimage helps make the transition, and the influence of a peer group and siblings greatly helps the development of these preimages. The child who is more isolated from peers and siblings must rely more on his family and extended family to provide him with the mental images of his approaching roles.

Normally, the child first anticipates and then progresses through a series of roles. There are series involving school, relationships with family, athletic development, work and chore responsibilities, and social relationships. In the social sphere the early puberty boy will picture himself beginning to socialize with girls in a new way, progressing to dating, courtship, marriage. The high school boy may conceive of himself as actively preparing for college, then attending college to prepare for a particular career, and progressing in that career through various levels of achievement.

The child's conception of progression through a series of roles is reenforced by his perception of his goal-oriented environment. He has seen his parents and others in his immediate environment progressing through various stages of development. Father moves from manager to vice-president; Mother from secretary of the PTA to president. With a thousand variations he sees those around him progressing through roles along innumerable different lines of activity. It seems very feasible to the child that, as a matter of course, he too will progress through more and more desirable roles. And each new position carries the gratification of achievement. Social progress, changing values and styles may cause upheavals in the directions role development may take; but some new role expectancy must replace whatever is discarded, or problems ensue.

The progression of this series of roles is never a smooth

and painless process. There are various crises concerning the achievement of new stages of development; toilet training, starting school, and adolescent rebelliousness are some of the normal crises that child and parent must cope with. Most crises are mild, and their resolution often leads to the development of new strengths. Some of the crises may be more serious and lead to major personality disruptions.

The importance of this progression through a more or less predictable series of roles cannot be overemphasized. Of course, it serves society's need for an orderly transfer of knowledge, responsibility, and authority from one generation to the next. The entire existence of the species, for example, depends on the development of individuals who understand, and are willing to assume, the role called "parent." The individual passes through innumerable earlier roles on the way to developing that concept. The progression through roles continues all through life: "I conceive of myself as the parent of an infant; there is much I must do," might eventually become "I am a fairly wise senior member of society; I must do what I can to mediate between my children and my grandchildren." It is clear how society benefits from the development of these roles.

The individual also gains a great deal in his personal development from these roles. The fact that each individual accepts, works for, and even fights for their attainment indicates how important they are. *That importance involves the individual's ability to maintain his self-esteem.* Where his expected roles are clearly laid out for him by his family and society, he can maintain his self-esteem by attaining goals that lead to the successful mastering of each new role. In time, and after innumerable encounters with the values of the significant people around him, the child internalizes these values. If they are definite, reasonably complete, and attainable, he has developed an internal mechanism for supplying a lifelong sense of purpose, direction, and self-esteem—manifestations of a sense of identity.

The ideas of stages of development, goals, ideals, and role images are all facets of the same phenomenon. They are aspects of the heritage each generation offers the next as a kind of "road map" for a meaningful and satisfying life progression. Some parts of this heritage are strongly identified with, some less strongly, and some repudiated completely. Sometime after childhood, between adolescence and adulthood, a very complicated process must take place: out of these various identifications, the interaction with society, and the individual's own psychological development and endowments, an *identity* must develop. The concept of identity implies more than simply the sum of what the individual has identified with previously.

The achievement of a healthy sense of identity involves a cohesive blending and accepting of the various internalized ideals and role images, as well as a feeling of acceptance of his new adult self by his environment. The result is a sense of security about one's place in the world and a confidence about the future.

Where there are circumstances that interfere with the development of a healthy sense of identity—such as when there have been major changes in the social milieu which make his previous role conceptions irrelevant—a serious crisis may occur described as *identity confusion.* Particularly damaging for the individual is the fact that his means for maintaining self-esteem through meaningful effort is seriously impaired. He may become depressed, preoccupied with a search for instant gratification, or angrily act out his frustration against society. Any of the old neurotic conflicts may be reactivated through a complicated regression to childhood problems that are preferable to the adult state of misery. There may even be a major withdrawal into the private world of psychosis.

These identity problems also involve conflict, but here the conflict is between the individual and his society, as well as between conflicting role images and ideals within the individual. He is confused about who he is and his relationship to his society. The result may be any manifestation of mental illness including symptoms of the classical neuroses. What is unique is that the stress which begins the process is related to an identity crisis.

Psychiatrists are quite familiar with such problems in middle-class patients (and middle-class patients represent the majority of patients seen for psychotherapy). They are largely related to the tremendous changes that have occurred in middle-class social structure in recent decades. Notable among these changes have been greater personal freedom, a reduction in the influence of the family unit and the traditional values of society, and a tremendous increase in class mobility. These changes have produced confusion in the individual's sense of who he is and what his roles are in society. This is where the effect of affluence becomes of significance. The tremendous increase in personal wealth, and the corresponding increase in class mobility, has caused changes in people's lives undreamed of a few years ago. Formerly, members of the middle class could expect to remain in a socioeconomic status similar to that of their parents, as would also their children. The roles that they learned, and the values associated with them, were highly adaptive to the world they lived in and thus quite stable. All that has now changed.

Children of middle-class parents can be reasonably certain that their social milieu will be considerably different from that of their parents. Increasing technology and social mobility virtually guarantee that each new generation must adapt to tremendous change. The social values and ideas of role progression that served the parents so well may be completely inappropriate for their children. These values and ideas of role progression vary with each gradation of social status. For example, with increasing family wealth the individual's actual need to be concerned with thrift and the preparation for future security decreases.

Children caught up in such rapid changes in their socioeconomic environment discover that the values they were taught at home are not appropriate to the society they are living in. Ideas concerning industriousness, thrift, honesty, and working toward future goals come into conflict with the ease of obtaining material gratification, duplicity in the behavior of those formerly honored, and a pessimism about the future of society that makes striving for future goals seem meaningless. The result is more a state of confusion than neurotic conflict. The universal sexual and aggressive conflicts are still present, but they are eclipsed by a feeling of hopelessness and alienation.

When there is enough evidence of serious personality disruption, such individuals may be referred for psychiatric treatment. The treatment involves an effort to resolve the areas in which the patient's family heritage conflicts with the realities of the actual society he is living in. There is usually considerable anger toward the parents for preparing him for a different world from the one he finds himself in. In spite of what often appears to be major confusion in one's sense of identity, psychiatrists usually find a basic core of middle-class values that have been deeply instilled.

There is a basic series of role ideas which can be adapted to the new realities. The concept of working hard to attain some meaningful goal is still there; the individual needs help in adjusting these goals to his new realities. While there are differences between his parents' teachings about sexual matters and the new liberalism of his peers, he still has basic ideas about a progression through a series of roles on the way to responsible parenthood. There is often a basic idealism and concern for others that can be built on as new sources of meaningful purpose and gratification.

The more rapid the accumulation of wealth has been, with all of its other associated changes, the greater the disruptions are likely to be. But as long as one is considering people who have concern about "getting ahead," improving their social status, and providing security for their future, one is still dealing with the middle class. And in spite of the various crises and disruptions that each generation may go through, there is a certain core of common values and ideals that can be adapted to new circumstances.

At a certain point in the acquisition of wealth, the situation changes: there is a major discontinuity between the values and ideals of the middle and upper classes. Many who have made that major transition find themselves with a deficiency in their mental images of meaningful life roles. These are the disadvantaged children of the rich. This is of increasing importance because there is every indication that the numbers of people involved in such drastic shifts in their social situations will be increasing tremendously in the immediate future. What is now a problem involving a relatively few unhappy rich could well become a situation of major significance within the next few years.

5

DYSGRADIA

What happens when the circumstances of an individual's life situation do not foster the development of a clear concept of the roles that are expected of him? We have seen how important these roles are for the development and maintenance of one's self-esteem, and so we would expect serious problems in that area. Among a group of the very wealthy such a situation is surprisingly common. They suffer from a unique form of identity problem.

These unfortunate rich children are impoverished in the development of their role images. They suffer a deficiency disease. There are great gaps in their mental images of progression through various roles from here (a role as a child) to there (some concept of an adult identity). These gaps do not represent the difficulties so often encountered in middle-class children as they pass from one role to another—for example, the normal identity crises encountered on the way from childhood to adolescence. Nor is it the same as the more serious state of identity confusion. These deficiencies in role conceptions are massive. To describe this situation I have coined the term *dysgradia,* meaning a disorder in stepwise progression. I have referred to children of the rich suffering from it as CORs. The concept of dysgradia has proven a useful tool in understanding and treating this kind of problem.

The CORs are usually not deeply involved in problems of identity confusion because they have not been exposed to roles that conflict with their actual life situation. Aside from vague feelings of unhappiness and emptiness, their absence of role images may not produce any difficulties within their familiar social milieu. They can live fairly comfortably without clear goals. The tremendous wealth makes material gratification so available that the emptiness can often be almost hidden.

The term dysgradia is intended to describe a particular form of identity problem rather than a specific form of emotional illness. There is a serious impairment in the sense of identity due to the deficiency of adequate role images. The individual, however, is usually not involved in great turmoil or confusion. The only indication that something is wrong may be a vague feeling of emptiness and unhappiness. Of course, crises may occur, especially when circumstances force the COR into confrontations outside of his protected world. Then the suffering may become severe, and some form of mental illness becomes apparent.

How does the transition from the middle class to positions of great wealth cause the breakdown in the passing of one generation's heritage to the next? The life-style of the rich creates certain circumstances which strongly predispose to dysgradia. The homes are usually large and isolated, so clusters of peers are less likely to congregate to exchange information. ("Gangs" of children, of course, do not guarantee good mental health—they may, in ghettos for example, reinforce criminal roles.) The absence of peer groups removes one source of needed information about future roles.

The presence of servants is also a problem. A certain portion of the rearing process is delegated to the household staff —too often a considerable portion. The attitude of the servants toward their young charges is variable, but they seldom have the same expectations that parents have. And the expectations of the parents are normally the foremost source of the child's self-expectations. The servants may see their wards as creatures to be served, without any concern about their preparation for future roles. They also may gratify their own unconscious fantasies of eternal childhood or act out their hostility by treating the children as crippled royalty. It is also a fact that servants may indulge their perversions with their wards.

The wealth of the family is in itself a deterrent to healthy role-image formation, especially concerning education and work. There is certainly no apparent need to be concerned about preparing the children to provide a livelihood for themselves, and so the children are left with blank spaces between being an indulged child and the idea of going off to do something meaningful each day. Education becomes less important as a means for providing for one's financial security, though it may be valued for itself or for social ends.

The more relaxed attitude about sex encountered in upper-class society has drawbacks as well as advantages. While the analysis of upper-class patients reveals fewer of the sexual inhibitions and conflicts more typical of middle-class patients, sexual relations seem to have been reduced in importance. Lovemaking is no longer the end result of a progression through a series of roles (dating, going steady, serious involvement), and in turn the beginning of a new sequence (engagement, marriage, parenthood). While in present-day middle-class America the old traditional sequences are being questioned and perhaps altered, the deterioration of these role sequences is much more marked for the upper-class youth. Sex for him is a readily available diversion, not necessarily signifying much more. This of course has a detrimental effect on marriage and child rearing.

In the sphere of marriage and child rearing, dysgradia exerts its most damaging effects for the individual and for society. There is little conception of the need to prepare for marriage; there is no gratification in pursuing and winning a girl since the COR's wealth makes him highly desirable, and he derives no satisfaction from preparing himself to provide for his bride. There is no concept of progressing through a necessary and challenging series of roles before marriage can be considered. Marriage is thus diminished as an indication of having successfully mastered a series of tasks and as a reason for enhanced self-esteem. It is often entered into without the more typical middle-class excitement. This reduction of the potential for marriage to be a source of great satisfaction, and a continuing means of maintaining self-esteem (as new roles are achieved), soon produces boredom, and the marriage is in trouble.

There are serious gaps in the mental images of the parental roles. So much of their own care was handled by servants that the CORs often literally do not know what to do with their children—except to turn them over to servants. The gratifications of mastering a series of parental roles as the children present new challenges are absent. The satisfaction of having children is reduced and the children in turn suffer.

The degree to which a child has developed the needed set of role preimages can be readily ascertained by brief conversations with children. A typical conversation with a healthy upper-middle-class eight-year-old might serve as an illustration.

"What does your dad do?"

"He's a lawyer."

"What does a lawyer do?"

"Oh, he makes up papers people sign when they have some business with each other. And sometimes he goes to court—but he doesn't have anything to do with gangsters."

"And what do you want to be when you grow up?"

"I think it would be fun to be a lawyer like my dad—even to work in the same office. But I love to take things apart—and Mom says that means I'd make a good engineer. She says I can decide when I'm in college."

Whatever this child does with his life, he has already identified with the ideas of a life's career, a freedom of choice, and the need for education. And he clearly derives gratification from anticipating his future. These basic ideas are often lacking in the children from certain segments of the very rich. A conversation with such a child might be startlingly different.

"What does your dad do?"

"Oh he sails and plays golf. Sometimes he and Mom go to France to live for a while."

"I mean, how does he get the money to do those things?"

"I think that comes from the bank."

"What do you want to be when you grow up?"

"I want to go to France."

Do these conversations seem exaggerated? Try these questions on some youngsters with varying backgrounds.

In many respects the lower-class child and the upper-class child are both more likely to suffer from serious degrees of dysgradia than the middle-class child. Brief conversations with these children will often reveal the extent of their impairment. During the adolescent years, a wide variety of diverse forms of impairment may not be as clear as before or after that period of turmoil. There are certain role changes that are biologically determined during adolescence and that may develop in an apparently normal manner, in spite of serious gaps in other phases of role conceptualization.

The approaching development of sexual maturity leads to certain goal-directed activities such as learning to dance or developing other social skills for attracting the opposite sex. For a period of several years, the youths from the various social strata may come to resemble one another more and seem to have an organization for their energies. However, the basic ideas for a meaningful life plan must be laid down well before adolescence commences. The dysgradic adolescent may blossom for a few years only to come abruptly to a crisis of absent purpose when those years have passed.

Children between seven and eleven will often give the most lucid descriptions of their internal state of affairs. And over and over one finds that the very rich and the very poor have the worst deficiencies. As a result of these deficiencies there are serious problems in maintaining self-esteem and providing internal sources of gratification.

In trying to understand certain aspects of emotional problems, one may search in vain for major areas of neurotic conflict or identity crisis. It is only when the deficiency of role images is understood that certain of these situations begin to become clear. With the description of the problem of dysgradia, we can now return to the discussion of Brewer.

Brewer was fortunate in that he loved his father and had some identification with him. But this identification was with a powerful, successful man; there were no internal images of a man working toward becoming something. There were ambivalence and major areas of conflict, but these could be resolved. His difficulties at college were in part the result of his dysgradia; everything had come easily and effortlessly to him up to that time. His natural endowment in intelligence and athletic ability enabled him to fall naturally into positions of high achievement. In the college situation, for virtually the first time in his life, he was called upon to enter roles for which he was completely unprepared. Not only could he not conceive of himself as a hardworking student, but even more tragically he had never developed a capacity for deriving pleasure from such a role of hard work and competition. Without a capacity for such gratification, he fell back to earlier, more primitive methods: the role of a little boy for whom driving a car and spending money like his rich father seemed the ultimate in achievement.

He had learned trust in his analysis; he learned to love in his relationship with Claire. Once I realized that I was making the mistake of expecting him to follow my ideas of middle-class roles before I would be satisfied that he was making progress, I was able to accept him for himself. He could now give and receive love, so he need never regress to the infantile searching for self-satisfaction. I also realized something else: his identification with his father in terms of the role of an effective, successful businessman could be fulfilled in spite of the absence of the preliminary goal-oriented identifications.

Foreign as the idea is for those of us imbued with the middle-class ideas of progression through stages to a career goal, that is not the only route to a gratifying and productive life. Just as the heirs to thrones once assumed the regal position when their time for succession arrived, many of the children of the rich are quite capable of assuming highly responsible positions. They cannot live up to the middle-class ideas of progression through intermediate steps. This was part of Brewer's problem: he was expected to assume a series of intermediary roles, whereas his upbringing had prepared him only for succession to the throne.

Once these ideas became clear to me, I felt more hopeful about Brewer's future. His natural ability, the resolution of his neurotic conflicts—not to mention his own considerable wealth—would enable him to find a position where his ability for leadership, and his ability to assume power could be advantageously channeled. Claire helped him establish some direction in his life. Had it not been for her, his analysis might not have turned out so well. I now feel that in addition to the analysis of conflict areas, more can be offered such patients by a more flexible therapeutic approach which includes attention to the identity problems.

Brewer's analysis and life experiences, together with his natural endowments, led to a reasonably happy result. Wilson was a much more pathetic figure.

6

WILSON

Wilson was born when his father was fifty-five and his mother forty-six. Needless to say he was not a planned child. There were already three older brothers from twenty-one to twenty-five. His father had amassed around twenty million dollars through real estate development and was quite ill when Wilson was born. It would appear that Mother anticipated the early demise of her husband and turned most of her attention to this new male in the house. As it turned out, Father lived until Wilson was seventeen. Because of his ill health, the active running of the business was turned over to the three older brothers as they completed college. They were very competent, and the enterprises flourished.

Wilson grew up with a doting mother and a father convinced he could die at any moment. His young son became the great pleasure of his life, and for those seventeen years he showered Wilson with everything money could buy. Wilson's home was every bit as impressive as Brewer's, though there were fewer members on the household staff. Mother loved to cook and care for Wilson, and Father enjoyed gardening; one or two maids were all that were needed.

His days should have been heaven on earth—being with his parents all day, outings to amusement parks, lunch every day at fine restaurants, toy stores, toy stores, toy stores. Almost every day he would come home laden down, his arms full of new toys. Dozens of electric trains, bicycles, models, games. As one might expect, he never seemed to value any of his possessions very much. Each new acquisition meant as much to him as a huge plate of food would near the end of an immense feast. And yet he cried for each new toy that caught his fancy.

He had become aware very early how much he meant to his parents. They beamed and bubbled with pleasure at each new gift they bought him. Their happiness became his happiness. He was bored with toys, he'd break them or throw them in a closet. The big treat was to go riding with Mother and Father and *buy* toys. Their pleasure was extremely exciting to him. The one thing he could do to give his parents pleasure was to let them buy him toys. His role in life was a child making his rich and elderly parents happy.

That became virtually the only source of gratification available to him over which he had any control. Nothing else was expected of him. In a tragic sort of way it became necessary for him to demand more and more toys in order to endeavor to recapture that feeling of satisfaction in making his parents happy. He received no true love from his parents; in a sense he was a toy for them—wind it up and it makes you happy in your old age. Because they expected nothing of him, he never learned any capacity for deriving gratification through his own achievements.

He did well enough in his schooling; Father and Mother wanted him to graduate from college and their joy at his (barely) passing marks was almost as great as their joy at his (contrived) pleasure at some new toy. As he grew older, the toys continued but became more complex and expensive —motorcycles, skiing equipment, elaborate camping gear (never used), a collection of antique *and* sports cars, more clothes than he could use in a lifetime. When nothing new was forthcoming for a few days he would start combing camera shops, sporting goods stores, car dealerships, and whatever else caught his fancy, until he discovered something that he absolutely *needed*.

Summers he would spend a few weeks on an uncle's ranch in Montana. He loved horses and would ride with the ranch hands for hours. One old foreman took him under his wing and kept him busy all day. The family marveled at how hard he worked and how well he took criticism. He secretly hungered for someone to treat him like a man and expect him to act like a man. Unfortunately, that exposure was too little to alter very much the damage that was already done.

When Wilson was seventeen his father died. He cried a little but his life changed not at all. He remained at home with his mother, and the toys continued. She would sometimes speak of his going to work, but always in completely unrealistic ways—being a banker, an architect—it was clear she wanted him home with her. He got a few girls pregnant, but they were only toys, and Mother took care of everything. Mother died suddenly when Wilson was twenty-seven. His parents had wisely set up a trust fund for managing Wilson's share of the inheritance, including his one-fourth interest in the family business.

I first saw Wilson when he was twenty-eight. In the year after his mother died he had gone to live with his oldest brother. He had been given a not-too-demanding job in the family business. He sulked, drank a great deal, fought with his brothers and their business associates, and filled his apartment with a mass of unneeded purchases. Their efforts to curtail his expenditures met with tantrums, and he was constantly fighting with the custodians of his trust (a bank) over their refusal to allow him one cent of principal to spend. The income from the principal he did spend represented a staggering figure.

The three brothers approached me, asking for advice on managing him. He was so much younger than they that they had had little to do with him as he was growing up. They were overwhelmed at this insatiable creature they found themselves responsible for. When he came in to see me he was indeed a pathetic sight. He was filthy and unkempt. He wore several expensive rings. His beautifully tailored clothing had apparently never been cleaned or pressed. He was plump and pink. I could see the handsome features of his brothers in him, only flabbier from too much food and too little exercise. There was a whine around his mouth and he seemed like a child holding back tears. He cried as he told me how badly his brothers were treating him. There was absolutely no insight into the bizarreness of his life. His only source of gratification was external—the acquisition of new toys; his brothers were interfering with his way of life. He was willing to see me in therapy. He seemed happy to have someone who didn't criticize him.

He came daily for three months and during that period complained constantly about his brothers and the trust managers.

"They wouldn't let me use my own money to buy a car," he whined.

"Why not?"

"They're so goddam conservative—five dollars over and they have fits."

"What kind were you thinking of getting?" I asked.

"A Ferrari."

"Aren't those rather expensive?"

"Oh, about eighteen thousand dollars—but I'm turning in the Porsche and Corvette—and they last so well I'll not need another for years."

His ability to rationalize was stunning! My efforts to explain their point of view were fruitless. He had no capacity for bearing frustration, he could not imagine himself in any role that involved service to others, the creation of products or capital, or any curtailment of endless material acquisitions. I wondered if pressure from a peer group—as in group therapy—might be more effective than I was being. He walked out of the group in a fury the first time they challenged his way of life and refused to go back.

I contemplated placing him in a psychiatric hospital where I could rigidly control his activities. His compulsive self-indulgence was a pitiful effort to obtain the only source of gratification he had ever known: the pleasure of his parents with their happy little boy. If I could frustrate this in a controlled setting what would happen? Would he become depressed, anxious, or even decompensate into a psychosis? I certainly didn't like the prospect of the last possibility, but it almost seemed preferable to the present situation. Sometimes when one decompensates under such circumstances, a healthier reorganization is possible. He listened in horror as I outlined this plan, then categorically refused.

At length I arranged a meeting with the brothers. I explained to them my understanding of how the present state of affairs had developed and the relative hopelessness I felt for any substantial changes. It didn't make much sense for him to continue living with one or another of the brothers; he disrupted their home life, and they were clearly not helping him. I suggested a plan that would spare them some aggravation and hopefully protect Wilson from getting into serious trouble.

A social worker advertised for a companion for Wilson. After a number of interviews she located a widowed retired army sergeant who was willing to take him on. He had something of the warm gruffness of the old ranch hand Wilson had been so fond of years before in Montana, and Wilson happily accepted the arrangement. They would share an apartment, and in return for quite a good salary, Sarge would spend most of his time with Wilson.

I would have one meeting a week with Sarge, and one

with Wilson. When Wilson went shopping, Sarge would go along and raise questions about whether Wilson actually needed this or that item. He would try to postpone purchases in an effort to help Wilson develop some capacity for tolerating frustration. Sarge would exclaim, "For godsake, you're gonna buy another camera?"

"Yeh, this is the newest—1.4 with electric film advance."

"Why in hell do you need that?"

"Well with 1.4 and Tri-X, I can take pictures indoors without flash."

"But you haven't taken any pictures at all in a year, and you have eleven cameras—I've counted them."

"OK, Sarge, what shall I do?"

"Let's think about it for a while—you can always get it next week—it's been in this window a month already."

"OK, Sarge, one week—now come on—I want to look at the quadrisonic stereo system next door."

The meetings between Wilson and me would give him a chance to ventilate his anger at Sarge, while I pointed out the wisdom of Sarge's advice. The meetings between Sarge and me involved mostly my persuading Sarge not to quit.

Our program has been going on two years. Wilson and Sarge go horseback riding several times each week, and this is practically the first pleasure Wilson has ever known that does not involve the purchase of something. When Sarge was ill with pneumonia a year ago, Wilson showed signs of really caring for another human being and was constantly at his bedside. That's where it stands now. Progress measured in inches, and yet better than nothing. Maybe another five or ten years.

Wilson is unusual in that many of his problems were

caused by the special circumstances of his birth—his parents' advanced age and his father's ill health. His story is included because he demonstrates several important points. First, not all children in the same family (rich, poor, or middle-class) will ever turn out the same way. Wilson's situation was an extreme one, but it is not uncommon that certain of the children are more exposed to growth-enhancing role images. His brothers were growing up at a time when Father was just amassing his fortune and were more closely identified with his middle-class origins. They also attended public schools and had one another and a large peer group to assist with establishing ideas of role sequences.

The brothers did not suffer any apparent dysgradia. Though Wilson's case was extreme, variations within families in which the children are much closer together are commonly encountered. Just as some children are sometimes singled out to be scapegoats, so also some are picked to "enjoy" the fruits of Father's success. (Usually the parents identify with this "lucky" child in a very special way.) This child may be the only one to show serious damage.

What kind of treatment was that for an analyst to prescribe? Hiring a wet nurse to help raise and wean him? Wilson was completely incapable of a more conventional insight-oriented therapy. He could not tolerate frustration, he had no patience, the work of acquiring insight offered him no reward. He had no interest in learning that he had bought his parents' love by letting them buy him toys. On this he blocked at every point. It was a choice of concluding that my patient didn't fit my technique, or of modifying the technique to fit my patient. Flexibility seemed the only way to offer Wilson some chance of growth.

7

PAMELA

Pamela's mother, Eugenie, was my patient. She was (and still is) an actress and a very talented and successful one. She was less successful in her roles as mother and wife. Four marriages, two suicide attempts, a brief encounter with drugs and lesbianism preceded her entering therapy with me. Surprisingly, I was the first psychiatrist she had ever seen; her very competent family doctor had seen her through the other crises.

When she started therapy her life seemed on a fairly even keel. She was a blond, beautiful thirty-eight—showing not too much wear for what she had been through. She carried herself like the famous lady she was, but without a hint of arrogance. She was actually frightened, lonely, and filled with grave self-doubts. Her fourth husband, Carl, who was thirty, seemed devoted to her and fond of Pamela who was a blossoming thirteen. Carl was her manager and was guiding her career wisely. He obviously loved Eugenie and this appeared to be the primary reason she entered therapy.

One must know something about Eugenie to appreciate what happened to Pamela. Eugenie's life had been almost a cliché of the Hollywood rise to fame. Her unmarried mother pushed her beautiful daughter from agent to agent from age ten on. Dancing lessons, singing lessons, acting lessons were all part of the routine. She was getting featured roles by the time she was seventeen—and earning them on the producers' couches.

She had acting talent and beauty and a pathetic quality that appealed to her public. She had known nothing but exploitation since she'd been a child. Her first three husbands were cruel to her in one way or another, but she had an unconscious need for abuse. The two suicide attempts were overdoses of sleeping pills when her second and third husbands left her.

Though Carl was kind and thoughtful, Eugenie hesitated a long time before marrying him. Soon after she did, she entered therapy for a severe depression. It was apparent that she had very deep feelings of guilt and inferiority and an unconscious need for punishment. The kind treatment she received from Carl was upsetting. However, our concern here is with the daughter Pamela.

Pamela was fathered by husband number two (though Eugenie wasn't absolutely certain it wasn't number one). She lived from the ages of one to five with number two, and from six to twelve with number three. From twelve on Carl was the father on the scene. I first met Pamela when she accompanied her mother for an appointment and we exchanged greetings in my waiting room.

"So you're Pam," I said. "I've heard lots of nice things about you." (I really had.)

"Thank you, Doctor," she said stiffly. An uncomfortable moment followed, during which she offered nothing more, and then she was told Mother would be out in a little under an hour. Eugenie didn't seem aware of the girl's stiffness. She spoke about what a good child she was.

"Pam is the great joy in my life—of course I love Carl—but Pam is special. She's always been a *good* child. Hardly even cried when she was a baby! My friends' children would cry and scream and get diaper rash—not Pam. She was never cranky or dirty. She even toilet-trained herself before she was a year! Never tantrums or colic. She'd sit and amuse herself for hours."

Eugenie knew she was illegitimate, and that was part of the reason she described herself as "damaged merchandise." She saw herself as dirty and valued only as an object for exploitation. Her fame as a sex goddess brought her wealth and recognition, but she was always ashamed of it; she felt sex was dirty and so was she. Her daughter became her hope for salvation. Her child, conceived in promiscuity as she was, would have a "clean life."

The communication between mother and child is subtle, delicate, beautiful, and unbelievably powerful. Was Pam, by her innate constitution, a quiet, contented child? Or did she sense her mother's need to have a "good" child? Did a fortuitous series of felicitous circumstances make for a remarkably smooth toilet training, or did the child understand that Mother felt conceived in dirt and famous through dirt and was desperate for her baby to be clean? The child got the message in some way, and she gave her mother what she needed.

Eugenie's pride in this thirteen-year-old overflowed. "She's never known any of the show-biz crap I grew up with—dancing, drama, fags, and dirty old men. She's a lady! Good schools, good friends in good neighborhoods, not a prude but doesn't feel she needs to gush over any guy who shows her some attention." I pointed out the dangers of overidentifying with Pam, but Eugenie replied that the girl had no problems. "Straight As for the past five years of school—class president twice! We've made a clean break with the past."

Eugenie's therapy was quite successful. She had the capacity for introspection and was able to understand her damaged self-image and the terrible masochistic search for punishment. We worked together for four years and she was able to make the transition from sex symbol to a more mature serious actress. Carl wisely guided her career, and her marriage seemed stable.

About a year after she finished her analysis Eugenie came to see me about Pamela. Pam was now eighteen and had graduated from an excellent private school at the top of her class. She had begun studying economics at UCLA, she was dating a bright young man, and all was well, except—

"I'm worried sick about Pam, Doctor. Remember the stiffness you commented on? Well it's become a thousand times worse. She's always polite to me and everything, and yet she seems so far away. She stares off a lot, and it often seems she doesn't hear me speak to her. Then there are days when she seems just fine."

Eugenie went on to describe some other disturbing symptoms. "At first I was so pleased she was studying economics, but now I'm sorry she ever started with it. She gets involved in theories and goes over and over them. I don't know what she's talking about most of the time. She writes rows and rows of numbers on sheets of paper, and screams at me—she's never done that before—if I touch anything." These symptoms of increasing emotional illness had been getting worse for two or three months.

I was about to leave for a vacation, and so I sent Pam to a colleague who I knew worked well with adolescents. By chance, I had an opportunity for close follow-up of the events which quickly took place: Pam's doctor and I met regularly on a research project and could exchange information. Also, I was doing some teaching at the hospital she was finally placed in and saw her on the wards and heard her progress reported at the weekly staff meetings.

Pam's doctor diagnosed a severe obsessive-compulsive neurosis rapidly decompensating into a psychosis. Within a few days she had to be hospitalized. I was startled to walk on the ward a few weeks later and witness this scene: Pamela was running down the hall, two nurses after her, shedding her clothes as she ran, and screaming, "Give it to me! Give it to me! Somebody screw me before I die!" She was sedated and placed in room seclusion with nurses around the clock. She didn't want to keep clothes on—if unattended a few minutes she would strip and lie masturbating on the floor.

She had grown into a beautiful woman resembling her mother, but less glamorous. Now she was disheveled, wild-eyed, and with lipstick and eye makeup heavily smeared on her face. This wild episode lasted only a few days, and she began calming down. Within another ten days she had become preoccupied with cleanliness. She washed her hands over and over until they were raw. She spent hours scrubbing the walls of her room. She wanted deodorant sprays and antiseptics. Gradually she returned to her preoccupation with numbers and economic theories. She left the hospital after a total of three months, returned to school, and continued intensive psychotherapy.

What had happened was a remarkable example of a mental illness produced by a severe state of identity confusion. Pam's basic image of herself was built upon a negative identification with Mother; like the negative of a film, what was black must be transformed into white. If Eugenie was dirty, Pam must be clean; if Eugenie had been promiscuous, Pam must be chaste and reserved; if Eugenie had little formal education, Pam must be a scholar; and if Eugenie was a sex symbol, Pam must be pure. And so Pam became to a remarkable degree the "good" child her mother wanted. This had started virtually from birth.

This self-image brought Pam gratification through her successes in school, praise from teachers, and admiration from her peers, but mostly from the extreme pleasure it gave her mother. There was all this gratification, but the price was high; Pam was more a caricature than a person. Her self-image was a rigid model with almost no room for any individuality. And as with any such rigid kind of role assignment, there was no room for growth; there was no series of role images that Pam could anticipate and progress through. She had to be good and clean!

In a sense, Pamela suffered from dysgradia. However, the problem was much more severe than simply a deficiency in role images. Pam was unable to develop a stable sense of identity because there was a serious absence of the identifications upon which an identity is built. Her early years with Mother had given her only fragmentary and conflicting images to identify with. There were memories of a drunken, painted mother involved with many men; there was an idealized image of a mother based upon the good fairies in the stories the servants would tell her; there was her perception of the good and clean role that was expected of her. These fragmentary images could not be formed into a cohesive identity.

The wealth of Eugenie contributed considerably to Pam's problem. Because of the seclusion of her huge estate, she was completely isolated from other children. From infancy on much of her care was turned over to servants who clearly understood Eugenie's obsession with having a perfect child. Because so much of her care was left to others while Eugenie pursued her career and romances, Pam had little opportunity to really know and identify with a mother. She probably would have been better off to have seen her mother as she really was and to know the struggle she went through to build a new life.

In addition to the problems produced by Eugenie's own emotional difficulties and the unfortunate effects of affluence on Pam's rearing, there was also the effect of the theatrical milieu they lived in. Because of her unstable personality, Eugenie could not resist trying to live the various images that were created for her by her press agents and fans. The result was that during the years Pam needed her most, Eugenie herself was severely confused about who she was. There was nothing whole and stable for Pam to identify with.

Under these circumstances, it is surprising how well Pam did. She should have fallen apart years before. But the pressures didn't reach the breaking point until college. There Pam was exposed to a freedom she was completely unprepared for. Each person could be himself and experiment with different roles. Pam knew nothing except "clean and good." The anxiety mounted as she became sexually aroused by her boyfriend, and she frantically plunged into her work. She had to keep herself occupied constantly to ward off the terrible anxiety of the realization that she was a nonperson. She had only one other possible alternative: the very distant and faded memory of Mother as a sex queen with many men around.

That memory was what she turned to as the "good and clean" image could no longer allay the panic. In the hospital she dramatized for those few days her childhood image of the only thing approaching a sexually mature woman she knew —the little girl's distorted view of her glamorous mother. She had nothing else to fall back on. Good and clean or nothing; and nothing produces a sense of panic that is unbearable and so starts a retreat from the real world into a psychotic search for some identity.

I have treated a few adolescents with somewhat similar problems; they are model children until their teens when their precarious equilibrium becomes apparent and serious disruptions occur. The gratifications promised by their peers for various experimental deviations from their family-sanctioned images cannot overcome the rigidity of these images. They have no concepts of themselves as basically good people, who can deviate a bit from home base and still keep their self-esteem. They feel they must either be perfect, or they might as well be dead. Sometimes there ensues a massive denial of everything they have ever believed in, and violent breaks with the family may occur. This, of course, is a common enough problem with all adolescents, not just the affluent.

Pam's case was, however, extreme. She is still in treatment years later. The process of arriving at a degree of flexibility in how she visualizes herself is laborious. She must come to know feelings and impulses that have been deeply repressed and integrate them into a newly evolving sense of identity. Eugenie returned for a brief period of further therapy to resolve her guilt about what had happened. She was punishing herself for trying to spare her child what she had experienced.

Understanding and acceptance of ourselves we need, and from insight hopefully the capacity to avoid the same old pitfalls; but guilt and self-punishment do little except to pay off our conscience so that we may blindly make the same mistakes over and over. Eugenie has suffered enough, and Pam is winning her fight.

8

AN OVERVIEW

THESE THREE CASES ILLUSTRATE SOME OF THE DIVERSE kinds of emotional problems that can affect the very wealthy. They all had some degree of the defect which has been termed dysgradia, but its relative importance varies widely in each situation.

Brewer had certain neurotic conflicts that had to be resolved—for example his distrust of women and his anger toward his father. He also presented a more or less "simple" case of a specific deficiency in his conception of who he was, where he was going, and the readiness for assuming intermediary roles along the way. The areas of neurotic conflict were not too severe, and many strong qualities were intact. It could have been a lot worse.

Sometimes one encounters situations similar to Brewer's, with one exception: The child is made into a scapegoat. The father says, "I've worked long and hard to get where I am, and that lazy kid has it all handed to him!" Perhaps the parents feel guilty for the neglect the child has suffered, and ease their consciences by focusing on the child's shortcomings. Sometimes they secretly enjoy his playboy mode of life, but for appearance' sake condemn it while offering no real alternative. Brewer escaped most of that.

Wilson is perhaps the most discouraging of the group, but representative in an extreme way of a very common problem. His whole life involved a childlike existence in which trips to "toy stores" of various kinds became his sole source of gratification. He became a subject for psychiatric concern only because of the extremity of his "toy-store fixation," and the concern of his brothers. There are many wealthy people leading lives quite similar to his, but within a milieu in which such behavior is not recognized as "sick."

Wilson could have met a much worse fate; as it was, there is a glimmer of hope. Suppose his family had not protected the financial security of his future. He surely would have spent every cent he had within at most a few years. He would then have turned to his brothers and, after exhausting their good will, become an outcast. I know of situations like this; the victim may commit suicide or become an eccentric mendicant, wandering down alleys looking for discarded toys.

Pamela represented a severe degree of mental illness which involved a personality structure weakened by inadequate and conflicting fragments of identification with her mother. While wealth certainly contributed to the problem, the show-business milieu probably had much more to do with it. But the inadequacies of Eugenie can be found in any social class. I know of situations in which the outcome has been much more grave; one young man with a background somewhat similar to Pam's also decompensated under the stresses of adult life demands, and was hospitalized. He did not make the recovery that Pam did, and eventually the family sent him to a state hospital. After fifteen years he is still there—a pathetic, confused child, with very little hope for recovery.

The serious personality disruption presented by Pamela, while unusual, has a parallel in cases seen daily by all analysts practicing in the Los Angeles-Hollywood-Beverly Hills area. These involve children of people in show business. Instead of the psychotic break with reality that Pam suffered, these children outwardly appear to be functioning quite well. But they share the same confusion in their identifications. Here are children whose parents play roles, they are actors in life. The children have difficulty perceiving who their parents really are and who they themselves are. Their famous parents are treated with a kind of awe far beyond that afforded any other group of the specially advantaged; on them are projected the dream fantasies of huge masses of people. Very quickly, with some notable exceptions, they are seduced into believing that they really are an elite.

Pity their children! Their parents are bigger than life and

certainly can't offer very attainable images for the children to aspire to. A few have enough talent to follow in their parents' footsteps and establish some kind of stability for themselves. Some are lucky enough to have good household help and to be isolated enough from their parents to develop a bitter but functional personality. Unfortunately many others turn in other directions; the three most common clinical syndromes I have encountered in show-business children are promiscuity and/or homosexuality, drug and alcohol abuse, and various varieties of sociopathic behavior (stealing, truancy, chronic running away, as examples).

The misuse of their sexuality is not difficult to explain. There is heavy emphasis on sexuality in the show-business world; it is a moneymaking commodity. The children are exposed to this constantly. Opportunity for gratifying experiences through a progression of life roles is not known to them; hence a turning to instant pleasure, instant approval, and instant—though temporary—reduction of the terrible tension of their directionless lives.

The drug problem is not unique to this group of children, but is complicated here by certain special circumstances. These children have money, and so the illicit drug industry has a profitable market. The problem of dysgradia leaves them with inadequately developed resources for obtaining gratification; that leaves them highly vulnerable to the transient feelings of self-satisfaction that drugs may supply. In addition, drug use offers an expression of defiance of family and society—an expression of their fury at having been cheated out of something they needed.

The antisocial kinds of problems are usually found to be dramatizations of the whole gamut of emotional malaise suffered by these children. Stealing is often clumsily executed and involves valueless objects; it is an expression of their feeling of deprivation and the wish for some token to which they attach some fantasy of value. One such child stole a lace handkerchief; only later did she realize it resembled a shawl Mother wore in her most famous movie role. She was searching for some part of an unapproachable mother she could hang onto. Running away and truancy, like the clumsy stealing, are also pleas for attention and concern—even if only punishment—and at the same time expressions of anger and rebellion.

The description of these young people, in some way suffering from some consequences of the show-business milieu, is of course incomplete and generalized. Each case represents a unique situation, with special circumstances setting it apart from the others. The parents are not the guilty culprits these descriptions may have implied; under the best of circumstances neurosis is the consequence of civilization. But problems, not unlike these, are seen every day in the consulting rooms of psychiatrists, and the show-business influence always seems to have had some harmful influence on the young person's development.

A special situation sometimes encountered has many of the characteristics of these problems of the affluent but does not necessarily involve wealth. It is the problem of the strikingly beautiful woman.

9

JUNE

JUNE WAS ONE OF THE MOST BEAUTIFUL WOMEN I HAD ever seen, and by far the most beautiful woman I had ever talked with. She was thirty-four, and had been urged to seek treatment by her husband because of depression. She was of Scandinavian extraction, with long blond hair, beautiful intelligent blue eyes, and perfect features. She was tall, shapely, and worthy of any man's choicest fantasies. And she was miserable.

She was assigned to me as one of my first treatment cases during my psychiatric training. The other residents quickly spotted her and began questioning and teasing me about her. When I decided she should be seen three times a week, they raised cynical questions about my motives. She was profoundly depressed and had strong thoughts of suicide, but I did look forward to our appointments. Even through her depression she was always beautifully dressed, made up, and perfumed. The early visits were spent in obtaining her history and establishing a working relationship.

She was born in a small midwestern town. An older brother died of leukemia shortly after she was born. There were no other children. The loss of her brother may have caused her family to treat her as special, or perhaps they too were awed by her beauty. All through her childhood she recalled comments about her attractiveness, and by her teens she knew she was a great beauty. She could recall virtually no difficulties during her childhood; her father and mother adored her and she usually got what she wanted.

June was an average student in school and was constantly pursued by the boys. She had learned that most women were very ready to be envious and hostile toward her, so she developed a friendly, nonthreatening façade which made her well liked by almost everybody. When she was sixteen she eloped with the captain of the high school football team. That marriage lasted about a year. June could give no reason for the divorce.

"We were terribly in love when we ran off. He was so handsome and so good to me. We both finished high school and then he went to work for his father who was a masonry contractor. There was plenty of money and he was never bad to me, but after a few months I wanted out. I can't give any reason why—I began feeling depressed—sort of like I am now, and started drinking a lot. I'd try and take an interest in our apartment—it was so cute—but I'd lose interest in it in a few days.

"I tried working as a secretary, but I couldn't type for any length of time without wanting to scream. I'd want to get out of the office and just drive around as fast as I could. The cops all knew me and never gave me any tickets—though they loved to stop me and flirt. I quit the job and tried staying home again. Then I started drinking pretty heavily and began hanging around bars. My husband just wouldn't get mad—he'd make the rounds after he got off work until he'd find me, then he'd bring me home and put me to bed. I don't know what I wanted—I just talked with the guys at the bar—never went home with any of them.

"I tried to have a baby—I thought maybe that was what I needed—but I've never been able to get pregnant. One day I just left for Los Angeles. He came after me, but I wouldn't go back. He kept trying, and wouldn't give up until I wouldn't even talk to him. Finally after two years he divorced me."

The difficulty in explaining the motivations for the breakup of that marriage was typical of June. She had been married three more times after that and had lived with many other men. None of the men was mean to her—they all seemed thoroughly captivated by her. But after a time she would become bored and restless and want to end the relationship. That was the only time she drank heavily, and that would stop when she succeeded in breaking things off. She had no great interest in money and, though her second husband had been very wealthy, had waived any settlement.

"I just reach a point where I've got to get out. And that's why I'm here now. My present husband, Ted, just keeps harping that I've got a problem and need help. I guess he's right—I have been through the revolving doors quite a few times—but right now it just seems I'm unhappy when I'm home with him and feel cheerful and relieved when I'm out. I started drinking so much he got our family doctor to give me some medicine that makes me vomit and want to die whenever I even sip wine. He puts the pill in my mouth each morning like I'm receiving communion.

"So now here I am. I can't stand staying with Ted anymore, I can't get away—he watches me like a bloodhound—and I retch at even the thought of gin. So lately the feeling of boredom is getting worse and worse—lately I started thinking about dying. It seems sort of scary-peaceful to take a bunch of pills—except Ted's thrown them all out—and just go to sleep forever."

Her depression was real enough, and she certainly needed intensive treatment, but her beauty stirred reactions in everyone she came in contact with. The receptionist would let me know June was in the waiting room by whispering, "Your Miss America is here for you." The other residents wouldn't believe she was as depressed as I told them she was—her appearance and ready smile made it difficult to convince them.

June seemed a little less depressed after a few months of therapy. We explored the realities of her life and she could find no reason for wanting to leave Ted. His only fault was not letting her go, and she could even sympathize with that.

"I can't seem to stay in love. Ted loves me enough to die for me. I loved him when we married, but now there's nothing. I don't dislike him—he's good to me. Doctor, I'm going to kill myself if I don't get out."

I increased her visits to five times a week and received word from my colleagues that they were absolutely certain we were having a torrid affair. But by then I was mostly worried about suicide and was contemplating hospitalizing her. One day I asked her how she always managed to look so well when we both knew how depressed she was. The answer was so frank it startled me.

"That's the one thing I've always had going for me—and, Doc, you have to capitalize on your assets, right? Since I was a little girl I've been beautiful—I'm not being vain—it's true, isn't it?"

I had to agree.

"Some people are brains, some have family names, some have money, me—I have looks. So I learned to make the most of it. You don't get traffic tickets, you get any job you apply for, you always have someone to buy you a drink—and something more—when you walk somewhere you know you're noticed and admired. I know your buddies pant over me—they probably rib hell out of you."

She wasn't sounding hard-boiled or conceited; there was a matter-of-factness born out of years of such experiences.

"I've never been so down I wouldn't dress sharp and make myself up. Without that I'm nothing and nobody. I'm no brain or anything. But I have a face and body men stare at and want. It's all I have and if I didn't have that I'd be dead. Since I was a little girl I could get out of assignments in school, avoid dirty work, get around people. You better believe I'm depressed—but you'll never live to see me without makeup."

Her beautiful blue eyes were wide and earnest, she seemed

almost panicky. I suddenly recalled that she was thirty-four —and though she was stunning, I realized she was losing her beauty. This woman needed men to fall in love with her in order to feel she was something of value. That must be the reason she had stayed with Ted this long—she was trying to break the pattern. She knew her years as a beauty were numbered and realized she had to settle with one man.

How could I help her? Her whole system of maintaining self-esteem and feeling valued was built on having men fall in love with her. Once she had them, there was nothing more in it for her. Then it was time to get a new one. At this stage in her life could she develop new ways of valuing herself?

"So that's why I always look good. That's my ace in the hole, my secret weapon—not so secret, is it? And with it I can get what I want. If I wanted you, I could have you—just like that." She snapped her fingers and looked closely at me.

If she had said that during the first few weeks of therapy, she probably would have seen signs of a struggle within me that she was looking for. Now I knew her too well for that: I was worried about suicide; I knew she needed men to fall in love with her but could not return love; and I felt pity for the dilemma she was in. She perceived enough of my reaction to know that something was different. She was frightened.

"You are beautiful—and maybe that's a big part of your problem. Therapy can help you, but you have to stay put for a while. No running away to new men, drinking, or eternal sleep." I tried to explain what I meant, but I felt she wasn't hearing me. She looked stunned. Another type of woman might have taken me on as a challenge. June had never needed to develop her seductive skills—any man was there for the taking.

She didn't keep her next appointment, and when I called

her home, Ted told me she had moved out during the night. He had no idea where she had gone, but he felt he would never get her back. I asked him to let me know if he heard from her, but he never did. I lost considerable sleep. Suicide? Had I erred terribly during our last hour? What could I have done better? Over the next fifteen years she came to my mind from time to time—especially when I'd see an exceptionally beautiful woman. Finally I had a chance to find out what had happened to her.

At a meeting a colleague told me he was treating her and filled me in on what had transpired. She had moved to Las Vegas and become mistress to a series of prominent men. The romances became shorter and more like business deals. She began using heroin and was soon addicted. She became a call girl and then a prostitute in a brothel. She had several hospitalizations for accidental overdoses, and numerous arrests. She was now back in California participating in a methadone maintenance program—a small, experimental project to control addiction my friend was connected with. She told him I had once treated her.

My friend wouldn't believe my description of her. She was now close to fifty and he said she looked sixty-five. Her blond hair was now white and disheveled, and her beautiful face was wrinkled and hard. She had had multiple bouts of peritonitis from chronic gonorrhea. She was on state aid and the only work she did was a little baby-sitting. As far as he knew she now had nothing to do with men. But she was alive and off heroin.

People who cannot maintain sources of gratification and self-esteem through the usual means are very susceptible to drug addiction. The drug shooting into their veins produces a momentary feeling of euphoria which resembles somewhat the exhilaration that comes with fresh achievement or with a new love. After the habit is established there is precious little of that euphoria, but brief periods of freedom from a terrifying, lonely anxiety.

What about the ordinary girl, the girl without overpowering beauty? What stages of development must she go through that June missed? The list would be extensive. From early childhood she would have to develop ideas about her course in life that were never necessary for June; sources of gratification would not be instantly available, they would need to be earned. She might take school more seriously, work toward recognition through various academic achievements ("I am a good student, preparing to become a nurse"). In her social relationships she might learn to obtain gratification through the development of close friendships ("I am learning to be a good friend—the girls trust me and the boys like my honesty"). She wouldn't be instantly thrust into adult sexuality; she would experience the maturing roles of little girl, preteenager, teenager, young adult, and the gratifications of mastering the challenges and crises of each stage of development.

June's story points up parallels and contrasts with the dysgradia of the rich. Like them, she had never developed a series of mental images of successive life roles that could represent a framework for a meaningful life. There was the euphoria of having someone fall in love with her, and when her beauty ran out, the desperate turning to heroin. To be loved for her beauty—no concept of being loved as a more total being—or to be high on dope were virtually the only sources of gratification she knew.

The children of the rich may use their money the way June used her beauty to obtain instant, though transient, gratification. But there is one significant difference: while the money may last a lifetime, the beauty will not. While time is kinder to some, physical beauty will surely fade. Most beautiful women are not as completely dependent as June was on beauty to supply a sense of worth. Many beautiful women resent being valued solely on their good looks and demand that they be judged as total persons. For them the passing of years represents the reaching of new levels of personal development, and not the catastrophe it was for June.

10

CHILDREN OF THE POOR

IN MANY RESPECTS THE CHILDREN OF THE POOR HAVE more in common with the children of the rich than either has with the vast middle class between them. Often the middle-class psychiatrist can understand—and perhaps help—the problemed poor more readily than he can the CORs. This is because in his training he has often worked in public hospitals and clinics where the poor represent a large proportion of the case load. He has often wrestled with the failure of the poor to fit into his middle-class stereotypes and developed some feel for the different kinds of problems they present. Hopefully he has also learned to modify his techniques to fit the needs of these patients. He has probably not encountered any very wealthy patients in his training and, once in private practice, most of his patients are middle-class.

Children of the rich have a tendency to suffer from an absence of a series of images of life stages that lend meaningful goals to their lives, the condition referred to as dysgradia. The case histories described have illustrated their poor adaptive methods of deriving gratifications from life. The poor, in many respects, have similar gaps in their images of their life movement. The absence of progressive role images produces a vacuum. Where there are no gratifying roles to aspire to, there can be no meaningful goals.

"The poor" of course covers a very broad spectrum. At the lower socioeconomic end the basic need for survival is paramount. The children of the very poor have no question about what goals have value; shelter and food are the primary necessities. To obtain them one needs either to work, steal, or obtain welfare. This simple preoccupation occupies the major energies of an appalling number of our people. Racial discrimination of course adds to the problem, and at times it seems deliberately contrived to keep their goals at the most primitive level.

Above this very basic level of poverty lies a huge number of poor for whom basic survival is not the main preoccupation. For this group there are goals above food and shelter, but these are distorted by the heritage of past historical events, as well as by present-day prejudices. Imagine a son of an unskilled laborer: his father is now off relief and working regularly as a janitor; there is enough income for a warm apartment and adequate food. Let's imagine that the income is not dissipated among more children than can be reasonably provided for. There is shelter, food, and some money left over for payments on a TV set, an occasional movie, and perhaps with the help of some charitable organization, a week in the woods at a summer camp for children.

What now to aspire to? For generations untold the beginning, middle, and end of life was occupied with the basic necessities of life. Survival was dependent upon fulfilling roles involving passive, obedient compliance to various masters. Now, though officially listed as poor, basic survival does not need to be the major preoccupation of the children. For most, while survival is assured, there is little racial, religious, or family identification to supply a framework of role images appropriate to a highly aggressive, competitive society. (A society, it might be noted, that is not too receptive to new sources of competition.) Without the capacity for deriving gratification through the satisfying fulfillment of meaningful roles, there is a strong tendency to turn to material symbols of success. For many this revolves upon one great ambition: to possess a status-providing automobile and certain other expensive possessions.

While a TV set was once a highly valued goal, it is now within the reach of virtually everybody. Color TV is on the ascendancy, but has not yet reached the pinnacle of desirability for the youths of the poorer classes. But the automobile has; there they can find the thrill of mobility, the distinction of highly individual styling, the power of huge engines. For the girls it has the phallic excitement of a rural tomboy's first

77

horse; for a boy, a loving mistress he can stroke, rub down, and show off to his peers. For many of the poor, an expensive automobile is about as far beyond basic survival as their aspirations have evolved to.

And here is one of the great deficiencies of our present-day society: once there is enough income to rise above the preoccupation with food and shelter, and move beyond the next stage—which often involves a preoccupation with material symbols of status—one finds a void. Beyond the car and a few other similar investments, society has not provided meaningful, attainable goals for the poor. A career, a home? Discrimination and economic realities tend to make that jump impossible. And so with increasing freedom from basic poverty, one sees a tendency toward bigger, gaudier, and more overpowered automobiles, and not much else of value.

The ability to place value on home ownership, education, and even the building of assets for the future is virtually unknown among large numbers of our poor. And here is a kind of dysgradia; a confusion about what to do with energy and money once they are freed up from basic survival. The absence of realistic, attainable goals produces a reservoir of envious fury ready to be attached to any cause that promises to supply some goal. The complete overthrow of the established system seems like a noble cause and on an unconscious level may offer some hope of instantly attaining the material achievements of the envied middle class. This reservoir of fury is subject to exploitation by those who would use it for their own ends.

A tragedy lies in the terrible failure of our society to help establish values beyond survival, automobiles, and television. Higher education, a desire for which has been awakened in recent years among minority groups, is seen all too often as a magical key to the rapid attainment of all the middle-class possessions. This of course leads to frustration and further rage. The idea of education as one important and difficult step in a whole series of steps leading toward attainable goals has not been developed.

Among the poor, a few simple questions put to children and young adults will often dramatically illustrate these points. I observed a brown-skinned Hawaiian boy sitting on a fence by a sugar mill chewing on a piece of sugarcane. He was watching the trucks from the fields unload their sweet cargo.

"What's your name?" I asked.

"Tommy, sir." He spoke the musical "pidgin" which is easy to understand after a short time.

"How old are you?"

"Nine."

We chatted for a few minutes and I learned his father was a fieldworker, they lived in a small house nearby, and his mother cared for his invalid grandmother. I asked what he wanted to be when he grew up.

"Well, I'm going to keep practicing the 'uke' and when I get good enough I'll get a job with the group that sings down in town. And when I make enough money I want to visit my auntie over Stateside. I sometimes think I want to be a singer, but my daddy says I should finish school and even go to college. I guess he's right. It would be fun to be an engineer in the mill."

He was a bright youth, with a love of music and some ambitions in that direction, but with a complete acceptance of the wisdom of a good education and an understanding that it can lead to responsible positions. He also had a curiosity for travel, fairly rare in large groups of lower-class children, and an idea of how he might progress to a point where he could earn enough money to satisfy that goal. One would predict relative freedom from serious conflict about his position in life.

A sixteen-year-old unmarried Mexican girl is in labor at County Hospital. She is wide-eyed with terror but relaxes a bit when her intern explains what is happening. She gives birth to a healthy son, and is smiling the next day when the intern and resident make rounds. The intern, who has an interest in psychiatry, comes back later the second day to chat.

The conversation reveals an appalling lack of knowledge about conception and pregnancy, and an effort is made to supply her with some essential information. After some rapport has been built, she is asked, "What are you going to do when you leave the hospital? What ideas do you have for your future?"

"Well, my mamma's gonna help me take care of my baby —she's had eight so she knows it good—and then maybe I'll get a job. We're on state aid now, and you can't live on that. I'm still pretty young and I want to have some fun."

She is asked about the baby's father.

"Oh, he don't want to get married. But I don't care much —I don't love him—it just happened. I think he got drafted or something. I got some boyfriends who are good to me. Maybe I'll work in someone's home—you know, take care of the house and baby-sit. If you get a good family, they treat you good, you have your own room, and maybe two days off a week. My friend, she has a job in Beverly Hills, her own room with TV, and they treat her like part of the family."

Her concept of life stages is certainly distorted. She has no clear idea of the sequence of dating, serious involvement, love, marriage, child rearing, and so forth. The pregnancy "just happened," and her mother will care for her child—she is already caring for two of her sisters' children. She has no definite ideas about ever marrying or hopes and plans for her child. She is aware of the necessity to work, but has no idea of advancement to more gratifying employment. The work she has in mind is simply an extension of family life—and a more comfortable kind of family than she has ever known.

This girl was attractive and could have realistically aspired to someday having her own family. She was bright and could have learned office skills so that she could provide better for herself than as a domestic. Instead she saw herself only as a child and sought the security of a new home where she would have her own room and TV set.

One more point must be made about this girl. She is quiet and sweet and can easily get work as a domestic. And, childlike as she is, she would be considered excellent in caring for children. It is a reasonable guess that her employers would be delighted watching her laugh and play with their children and would leave them with her with confidence. And while she would never knowingly harm any children, there is certainly a deficiency in the adult kind of guidance that children should receive from their caretakers. Hopefully the children's parents will make up for this deficiency. Unfortunately sometimes the quiet, happy situation of children playing with the domestic-child seduces parents into a less active role with their children.

The Hawaiian boy had fairly firm ideas for a gratifying

progression through a life that he had control over. The girl just described at least had hope for some gratifying attention from boyfriends and the gratifying security of an employer-family. At the lower portions of the lower class are those who are almost devoid of any conception of such gratifying modes of life, much less any control over their destiny. Ask a child from the deep poverty group what he wants out of life. He may describe some material things that he wants, but one can probe in vain for any sequential life plans.

There is no question but that discrimination has stifled opportunity. But the question remains: if opportunities were available, could they be properly utilized without a corresponding educational effort to develop ideas about utilizing these opportunities in organized, goal-directed ways?

11

THE GOLDEN GHETTO

ONE CANNOT HELP MAKE THE OBSERVATION THAT among the very rich there seem to be distinct groupings of life-style: those who seem busily committed to active, productive pursuits, and those whose main sources of gratification center on the self-indulgent use of their wealth. Few of the latter are ever seen as patients by psychiatrists, though considerable can be learned about them from their friends and relatives who are patients.

Suppose one has an inheritance of many millions of dollars that is managed by a bank and that produces large sums of money annually without ever depleting the capital. To the average middle-class person, the fantasy of such a situation would produce endless ideas for delightful ways to live. Surprisingly, for many who actually live in such a situation, their lives are boring, shallow, and stereotyped to an appalling degree.

This is a group that has a deficiency in ideas of gratifying life progression, and for whom the use of their wealth is the only tool—inadequate as it may be—that they can conceive of as supplying any pleasure in their lives. Among this group, the privileges of wealth are the only things that are valued. And this produces a stereotypy as uninspired as any lower-middle-class housing tract.

There is a hunger, wherever this problem exists, for sources of gratification; and when that gratification depends on things associated with wealth, the options become very narrow. A special life-style often develops among groups of such people. Some consensus must be reached among the particular group as to who may be admitted to their ranks. The prospective new member must possess the proper set of traits that have been decided upon as desirable, but above all he must have enough wealth.

People tend to avoid close contact with those who make them feel envious or ashamed. Thus the group under consideration would tend to avoid those who were actively working or engaged in some creative, productive endeavor; contact with them would tend to produce shame. The rejection of such a person would be rationalized in some manner, such as ridiculing their activities, or questioning whether they were truly wealthy if they chose to work. By this process, the group members come to resemble one another closely and to reinforce whatever values evolve.

The choice of where one lives becomes severely narrowed. A large, beautiful home in a magnificent setting may not be good enough if the group ideas of value are not met; being north or south of a particular street may become of crucial importance. There is a tremendous amount of envious copying; once something new has been sanctioned as valued by the group, there is a rush by the other members of the group to enjoy the fleeting feeling of gratification that comes with it.

Philanthropy often becomes an important diversion. One may contribute something to one's fellowmen—a feeling that may or may not be truly valued—while creating novel new opportunities for wealth-associated activities. Their philanthropic organizations are inevitably extremely selective, admitting only the chosen few and thus creating an illusion of value in belonging. The fund-raising activities must be elaborate and well publicized in the press.

Recreation becomes limited to certain group-sanctioned activities that are sufficiently expensive to be highly valued. Fox hunts, polo, and raising racehorses, while perhaps old hat, might fit the bill. Yachting is acceptable if the boat is expensive enough and the yacht club is restricted enough. Skiing is sanctioned, providing one has the proper equipment and skis at the proper resorts.

Travel becomes restricted, not because of any dearth of exclusive resorts, but because each small subgroup must stick closely together to reinforce one another's feeling of value. There is no true sense of freedom that should come with great wealth. The members of the group are truly frightened to venture very far outside. They are uncomfortable with the working classes who make them ashamed, and whom they must devalue. They are ill at ease with strange groups of very rich who might be even more affluent than they or who might share a different set of values. They are trapped in their golden ghettos.

Constricted so severely in their way of life, a terrible boredom sets in. Alcoholism is very common. Marriage and divorce are pursued at times with near-desperation.

The pleasures of child rearing are often virtually unknown. The satisfaction of comforting a sick child and making him feel better is left to the servants. Since their lives required no particular preparation for survival, they do not have the pleasure of fantasizing about the great things their children will do. The great pleasure that most people derive from helping their children achieve goals is also lacking. Children are additional beautiful possessions that the group may sanction as valued. But sacrifice, planning, suffering, and sharing in achievements are not part of the value system.

While the foregoing may sound like an exaggerated indictment of "the idle rich," it is an accurate description of the way of life of a surprisingly large number of people. They cannot be considered ill in that as long as they avoid exposure to the outside world they are free from anxiety, and as long as the group functions smoothly, enough new pursuits are sanctioned as valued to keep the boredom at a tolerable level. This is clearly not a very gratifying way of life, but can be surprisingly stable. When there is a casualty it is often due to unusual circumstances such as some outside influence. This was the case with Cleo.

12

YOU CAN'T SAY NO TO ME!
The Story of Cleo

CLEO WAS BORN AND RAISED ON A BEAUTIFUL ESTATE IN Connecticut. Her mother had inherited a large share of stock in a corporation her grandfather had founded. Her father had large holdings of cattle land in Texas. The main house was huge and there were seven servants. Her upbringing was typical of the more unfortunate children of the rich: most of her routine care left to servants, she was delivered to her parents for their diversion when she was spotless and doll-like.

Cleo—an only child—spent most of her time under the watchful eyes of the servants, and as she grew older she attended an excellent private school nearby. Her parents had virtually nothing to do. They clung closely to their small circle of friends and stayed carefully within their golden ghetto. Over the years their drinking increased to the point where they were borderline alcoholics. They had their first drink at 10 A.M.—by avoiding anything earlier, they reassured themselves they were not problem drinkers. In the afternoon they both napped for several hours to sober up for dinner.

Dinner was always an ordeal for Cleo. She was bathed and dressed and delivered to her parents between their fourth and fifth predinner martinis. They fussed over her for a few minutes and then—after perhaps a few more drinks—sat down to a very formal dinner. They actually ate very little, but magnificent dishes were elaborately served. (After dinner Cleo would often beg a peanut butter and jelly sandwich in the kitchen.)

"Well, sweetheart, you look just lovely." Mother's speech was a little slurred and her bloodshot eyes were dull and uninterested.

"Thank you, Mother."

"How's school, Pumpkin?" Father wasn't aware school had ended for the summer.

"Just fine, Daddy."

Then an uncomfortable pause while Father and Mother finished their drinks. Dinner was served beautifully, although Cleo didn't know what many of the French dishes were and was relieved that her parents were oblivious to the fact that she ate almost none of her dinner. Conversation was always dull and repetitious. Cleo would stop listening and dream about the horse she'd been promised someday. She would imagine herself galloping across the countryside, watching trees and grass fly by. She would be returned to her surroundings with a start when her parents left the table and wobbled off to bed.

Cleo didn't think much about her parents or her life in general. She often daydreamed about horses. Years later she realized how deadly boring her parents were and how much she had resented their lack of any real attention to her as a person. She narrowed the sweep of her thoughts and feelings and managed to think and feel very little in an effort to avoid the pain of these feelings. Much of what she did was as if she were in a daze, reflexively performing what was expected of her. When her feelings came close to the surface, she felt great anxiety.

Shutting out thoughts and feelings worked quite well in preventing the breakthrough of painful realities. At times, however, her tension would build up and then she had to turn quickly to other methods of avoiding anxiety. Riding her fantasy-horse wildly worked for a while. So did sleeping. Clea slept an unbelievable amount of time. This was partly an identification with her parents who spent a great deal of time sleeping off their alcoholic excesses. The most damaging device to avoid anxiety involved her relationship with her nanny, Agatha.

Agatha was very, very proper and very British, and extremely efficient in performing her duties involving Cleo. But at night, when she put Cleo to bed, she would give vent to her pathetic, sick fantasy life. She would rub Cleo's genitals while telling her wildly exaggerated stories about the glamorous life of her parents.

"Go to sleep, Cleo, while I tell you about the ball your parents are going to at the club. They are going to have a hundred-piece orchestra playing in this huge ballroom. All the ladies will be in beautiful gowns and the men in tuxedos. Your mother's gown was handmade in China and has a thousand pearls sewn on it. Oh, you should see her in it! She's the most beautiful lady in the room. Everybody stops and looks at her when she comes in with your daddy. She'll wear a diamond tiara in her hair and all the other women will wish they could die, they'll be so envious."

Cleo would listen in a kind of stupor, her eyes glassy and her face flushed with overstimulation, picturing the fairy-tale scenes that Agatha painted for her. Cleo knew there was something wrong with what Agatha was doing, but it relieved the awful tension she felt. It also supplied her with alternatives to the drunken, sleeping, unconcerned parents she saw; in Agatha's world they traveled and danced and did glamorous, exciting things. This nightly ritual went on until Cleo was fifteen years old. One night she pushed Agatha's hand away and said, "No more of that, Agatha." Agatha nodded sadly, and left the next day.

Cleo did well in school. She could take an assignment and do it beautifully. She could memorize very well, and learned French, German, and Spanish easily. She could not, however, think in a creative manner. She could repeat what she had learned, but she could not express original ideas. When asked for her opinion, she would supply something she had read or heard, but nothing of her own was forthcoming. She was so bright and well informed that this deficiency in the ability to think for herself went almost unnoticed by most of her instructors. An exception was Miss Cook, a contemporary history teacher.

"What do you think about the Tonkin Gulf Resolution?" Miss Cook asked.

"Senator Mansfield said—" Cleo began.

"That's not what I asked," her teacher snapped. "What do *you* think?"

"President Johnson said—"

"Cleo, what is *your* opinion?"

"I think . . . I think . . ." Cleo began trembling and she felt dizzy. "I think that the President should—the papers—I think . . ."

Miss Cook saw that Cleo was on the verge of screaming and let her sit down. Later, in her office she and Cleo discussed what had happened.

"I'm sorry I pressed you in class," she said, "but I've noticed that you never seem to express your own opinion about anything."

"I know that," Cleo admitted, "I always get blank when I try to decide how I feel about something. I really try, but nothing comes. I've never talked to anybody about this before. I can't decide how I feel about anything. I don't know whether I like certain people or not—I just go by what other people say. I don't even know what I want to take in college. I'm good in languages, so my advisor suggested I major in one of them. But I don't know if that's what I want, or which language, even."

Cleo began to cry. "I don't know whether I want to date a particular boy or not! If someone asks me out I usually stall him off for a few days while I check on what the other girls think of him."

Miss Cook realized she was dealing with a serious problem and, after offering some reassurance, dropped the subject. Cleo was quick to compose herself and went off in her usual cheerful manner.

Cleo was a very pretty girl—pug nose and large dark eyes, a beautiful blend of her Irish-Italian background. She was popular with the boys but had a reputation of being hard to get. This was actually a result of her difficulty in deciding how she felt about anything. She was easily influenced by anyone who was persistent and dominant. Just as she had been submissive to her parents and Agatha, she tended to respond similarly to the people around her at school. She enthusiastically adopted the views of forceful teachers; she would write compositions for girls who asked persistently enough. She would accept dates from boys who were the most determined. As a young girl the tendency to not think, to sleep her life away—either in bed or walking around in a sort of daze—had been adaptive; it had helped her endure a miserable childhood. But this tendency to not think for herself persisting into young adulthood now caused her some problems.

Cleo visited Miss Cook a half dozen times during her senior year. She discussed how blank she felt when she tried to think about her opinions on anything. Her grades were straight As and yet she felt like a well-programmed computer—excellent at retrieving and processing data, but incapable of actually thinking. She was going on to a university with a major in French but had no real feeling that that was what she wanted to do. Her greatest distress concerned Ward, a young man who was pursuing her vigorously.

Ward's family was as wealthy as Cleo's, but led a very different kind of life. They were involved in multiple business activities and dabbled in politics. Cleo was intrigued by the much more interesting kind of life that Ward and his family led, but she was also very uncomfortable with it. She had grown up in her family's golden ghetto and naturally assumed that her own life would follow the same pattern. If Ward, through some quirk of fate, had not decided that Cleo would someday be his bride, chances are she would have married one of the young men in her family's circle of friends and never had to suffer the terrible pain that awaited her in the next few years.

She told her teacher-confidante how uncomfortable she was with Ward, but how she was unable to refuse his invitations. At one point Miss Cook gently suggested some "counseling"—a euphemism for psychiatric treatment. Cleo was very receptive. But her family simply said, "You aren't crazy," and Cleo completely put it out of her mind. At the suggestion of her parents, she did not pay any more visits to her teacher.

Why was Ward so attracted to Cleo? She was truly lovely, but most boys at school did not pursue her for long. They found her rather "flat"—able to be witty and fun and obviously intelligent, but with a shallowness and lack of originality that became wearisome after a while. Ward was a very manipulative young man. He knew exactly where he was going and what he wanted in life. He was going to be a corporation lawyer, become active in politics, and eventually run for public office. He needed a wife who was attractive, intelligent, made a good public impression, and could be molded into whatever he wanted. Cleo suited his needs perfectly.

They attended the same university and after two years were formally engaged. Cleo sometimes felt trapped and wished she were free of Ward's domination, but she always quickly put such thoughts out of her mind. Ward led her into school politics, and in their senior year he was class president and she was secretary. Cleo hated the politicking, she dreaded speaking in public, and was grateful that all her speeches were written by Ward. She longed for the simple, safe life she had known at home: the few familiar friends, the club with its comfortable social events, the familiar vacation spots.

They spent Christmas with Cleo's family. Ward was charming and was quickly accepted by Cleo's family and their tight little circle. But at the Christmas party he confided his disappointment in them.

"They're nice people—but so *ingrown*. They all have plenty of money but really don't know what they *could* be doing. Not one of them is known in the state, none are on the governor's advisory commissions or anything. They could exercise great power in this state, but they just sit at that stupid club and drink. None of them can do us any good."

Tears welled up in Cleo's eyes. "Ward, those are the people I've known all my life. They're good people and . . ." She knew she deeply resented Ward's attack on what had always seemed a most pleasant group of people, but she was unable to muster a very convincing case for their worth. She also felt a flash of anger at his opportunism, and this made her slightly dizzy.

"Ward, you act as if the only thing you care about in people is whether they can help your career. I don't think—"

"That's right! You don't think when it comes to my career.

I'm taking care of that, and your duty is to give me whatever help I need. It's a dog-eat-dog competitive world we're in, and it's power that counts. I never want you to think of interfering with my goals." Ward's harshness was abruptly turned off, and he wiped away Cleo's tears and tenderly kissed her. "Now smile and have a good time." The dizziness persisted, and for a fleeting moment Cleo saw herself galloping across a field on a beautiful stallion. Then she felt suddenly calm, smiled, and had a good time.

Easter was spent at Ward's family estate and she was jolted by the differences. His father, Ward Senior, was active in business and was constantly on the telephone, in conferences with associates, or flying to New York. Cleo wasn't sure what it was all about, but understood it had to do with interests in a brokerage firm and large real estate holdings. Ward and his father were close, and Cleo could see the pride in the older man's eyes at his son's outstanding success in school. Politics was a sort of family hobby, and Father was on a first-name basis with governors and senators.

Ward Senior watched Cleo closely for a few days and then announced, "Cleo, you're perfect! Ward couldn't have done better. From now on you call me Dad." Cleo again felt that slight dizziness. She didn't like the older man's comment; she felt like a piece of real estate that had been appraised and found to be a good investment. She was also aware of how much her relationship with Ward paralleled the relationship of Ward Senior and his wife Belle.

Belle was quietly beautiful and completely at the service of her husband. Cleo found herself thinking that Belle was as well trained as the servants. That thought surprised her—she usually didn't allow critical thoughts into consciousness, but Ward Senior's acceptance of her was frightening. Belle seemed like a puppet at times, a smile frozen on her face, and a complete lack of any sign of independent thinking. Cleo quickly put those thoughts away, but she had nightmares for a few nights, an indication that her ability to repress her anxiety-producing thoughts was weakening.

When the two women were alone Cleo noted that Belle continued to smile pleasantly and not betray a hint of loosening up. Only once did Cleo observe signs that the role was a strain for Belle. It was late at night and Cleo went downstairs to the study for a book she had left there. Belle was sitting in a chair with a tumbler of whiskey in her hand and a half-empty bottle next to her. The fireplace was blazing and Belle's face reflected the flickering red. Her expression was of unbearable pain. Cleo turned unseen and ran to her room. That night she awoke screaming from a dream.

It was a pleasant week of parties, dinners, and long walks in the woods alone. Ward was usually studying or traveling with his father. In the woods Cleo began to realize that she was terribly unhappy, that she was destined to play a role she hated. She had absolutely no idea of what she could do about it, but Belle's frozen smile haunted her. She was relieved to get back to school.

As she plunged back into the busy school routine, that brief awakening of self-awareness quickly receded. She simply did not have the emotional capacity to alter the direction in which she was being led. She and Ward had a large wedding that summer. Though she had nightmares for several weeks before the wedding, she was not conscious of any doubts about it. Her years of perfecting the defense of not thinking about her feelings spared her the tremendous anxiety of confronting a dilemma with which she could not cope.

The years passed rapidly as Ward attended law school and Cleo was a graduate student in French. Going into his senior year Ward was running unchallenged for class president and was editor of the *Law Review*. Cleo ran reluctantly but successfully for president of the graduate students' association. She was very effective in her schoolwork and administrative duties, but had brief moments when she realized that she was miserable. Ward was exuberant and busy most of the time, and quite unaware of Cleo's growing discontent.

Ward graduated from law school with highest honors, and entered a very prestigious law firm. Cleo received a master's degree in French and worked a few afternoons a week doing some translating and tutoring for college students. They now had a large townhouse, and Cleo spent most of her time losing herself in books. She often read four or five paperbacks in a day, and then reread them if her day's supply ran out before bedtime.

After three years Ward was a partner in his law firm and was growing more active in politics. He ran successfully for Junior College Board and was becoming somewhat known in the state's political circles. Cleo was constantly entertaining at home or attending affairs with Ward. She began suffering severe dizzy spells and on one or two occasions felt too sick to attend dinners with Ward. Ward sent her to a neurologist for a complete examination. The doctor's report concluded that there was no organic cause for Cleo's dizziness. Ward took that to mean there was nothing wrong with her and ignored the recommendation that a psychiatric consultation be obtained.

A few days later a crisis occurred. Shortly before a black-tie fund-raising dinner Cleo became too dizzy to stand up.

"Get up and get dressed! There's not a damned thing wrong with you!"

Cleo was fighting back a wave of nausea and answered, "No." Ward's face grew red and he grabbed Cleo by the shoulders and pulled her up until her face was a few inches from his. He said softly, "You can't say No to me." Then he lifted her to her feet and gently led her to her dressing room. Cleo dressed and attended the party.

For a few months Cleo thought very little about how she felt, but during the brief moments between devouring books she would have flashes of dizziness. There is a limit to how long and how thoroughly one can repress strong emotion and Cleo was at her limit. The words haunted her as she lay in bed: You can't say No to me—You can't say No to me—You can't . . . "Why can't I?" Cleo asked herself. There was no answer—she just knew she couldn't. If only she could sleep—but for the first time in her life that escape was denied her. "I can't say No, and if I keep saying Yes, I'll kill myself. I must leave."

Cleo left the house while Ward slept, taking only a small traveling case. She took a cab to the airport and then wandered around the deserted passages for an hour. She realized she was saying No to Ward but she had no idea what she wanted to say Yes to. Going home to her family was out of the question. During the years with Ward she had realized how pointless their life was, and the thought of going home brought up images of lying passively in bed while her nanny fondled her. She flushed at the memory of how pleasant that had once seemed, and she knew she could never live at home.

"Their whole life was like that," she thought, "lying in bed passively, or drinking at the club—it's all the same thing—living the life of an infant." She was beginning to think.

She studied the flight schedules. Her old history teacher, Miss Cook, had retired to the West Coast. Cleo took a plane to Los Angeles and at seven the next morning was at her door. As she rang the bell she realized that Miss Cook was the nearest thing she had to a friend. Miss Cook opened the door and without any questions led Cleo to the kitchen where she was making breakfast.

As they ate, Cleo struggled to explain her plight. It was difficult because so much of what was troubling her had never really been thought out in words. She groped and struggled and finally wept. "I must learn to think, and to say No, and to know what I want. Oh my God! I've got to know what I want for myself!" Miss Cook listened and seemed to understand better than Cleo did. She said, "Tomorrow we'll find a doctor for you." The university supplied the names of three psychiatrists, and that's how she came to see me.

She was poised and pretty as she described her need for help. It was impossible to let her tell her story spontaneously as is the usual custom; she needed many questions to help her along. She appreciated my summarizing what she was telling me—it helped her crystallize her confused unhappiness into words that described feelings and conflicts. We agreed to meet daily for the time being. After the third hour I received a call from Miss Cook. Ward had arrived at the door, packed Cleo's things, and led her to his cab. Cleo went silently and as if in a daze. Miss Cook was distraught and afraid that Cleo would commit suicide. She promised to keep me informed.

Cleo did not come out of the daze on their arrival home. She did not eat or speak but stared blankly straight ahead. After a few days Ward became worried and called the neurologist who had seen her previously. He said she had a dissociative reaction and arranged for her to be hospitalized at an excellent psychiatric hospital. She was there for almost six months. Each time Ward visited there was a setback and it was finally agreed that he should not come.

After several months Ward sent word that he was obtaining a divorce. As she read his letter, Cleo smiled for the first time since she had entered the hospital. She agreed with his view that she was not a suitable wife for a man in his position. She understood that he would rather have the political liability of a divorce to cope with than an unsuitable wife. In her therapy there she was learning to express the anger she felt toward Ward and her great fear of him. Though he was no longer a problem to her, she was aware that she was able to assert herself to only the slightest degree. She felt extremely vulnerable to any forceful person.

After she left the hospital, she returned to live with Miss Cook and resumed therapy with me. After a few months she took her own apartment and worked part time as a tutor. We met daily for a while, then gradually reduced the visits to weekly. We worked together for a total of three years.

Cleo suffered severe deprivation in the midst of great riches. Her family gave her very little love and interest, but supplied her with complete security as long as she was compliant and caused no problems. Her relationship with her nanny further encouraged this passivity. Unlike Pamela, who had virtually no conception of what her mother was really like, Cleo saw her parents quite clearly. At an early age she recognized them as indolent, shallow, self-centered people leading meaningless lives. She realized they were incapable of supplying her with parental concern and love, and her reaction was rage. In her therapy she recovered memories of this early rage.

This anger toward her parents had to be repressed; to the child such feelings are tremendously threatening. Frightening fantasies of destroying them led to fears of horrible retaliation or terrorizing thoughts of being left all alone to face certain oblivion. She had resolved this terrible conflict between her rage and the fear of its consequences by a massive inhibition of her capacity to think for herself and to react emotionally. The dizziness was a mechanism to block out her feelings when they came too close to the surface. The wildly running stallion in her fantasies was the last vestige of the little girl's protest. She turned to compliance and passivity for the little security and gratification she could obtain.

While she suffered from the lack of a conception of meaningful and gratifying life roles, her problem was much more complicated than simply dysgradia. There were major areas of conflict involving her anger at her parents as well as defects in her personality resulting from the lack of healthy people to identify with. Her effort to adapt by developing a passive, nonthinking character structure was very nearly fatal for her. Her hold on sanity was precarious, and when she entered the hospital she was very close to a psychosis.

The progress of any course of therapy is always difficult to describe. A more typical kind of neurotic conflict might have a course that could be described in more or less predictable stages. A problem like Cleo's requires a much more active participation by the therapist, and is more concerned with strengthening the ego—in many ways an educative kind of therapy—along with the more conventional concern with areas of conflict. Cleo developed considerable insight into the nature of her problem, but the step from insight to changes in her personality was an especially difficult one for her. Remembering and understanding the rage at her parents could not heal her seriously stunted mental functioning.

Cleo's sessions tended to focus on her day-to-day activities. There was a concern with her dreams, her memories of childhood, and an awakening of a more adult fantasy life. But mostly she needed help with her strong tendency to become passive with authoritarian people. She needed help learning to say No and looking to herself to discover what she wanted. Instead of lying on the couch while the analyst follows the free associations and observes the struggle between conflicting drives, a patient such as Cleo often must sit up, face her doctor, and patiently be helped to develop functions of her mind that were arrested in childhood.

Those of us who know what we want and who are able to know how we feel much of the time often have difficulty empathizing with people like Cleo. There is a tendency to grow impatient, to conclude that there is a vacuum which can never be filled. And indeed, after her period of therapy, Cleo was not what would be considered a "normal" person. She led a much fuller life, her emotional responsiveness was vastly increased, and she was much better able to express her wants. But there was a difference about her that remained: a cautiousness in her social relationships, a tendency to pause while she deliberately searched out her feelings when confronted with decisions.

She married a university professor who was also a rather cautious, quiet man. She obtained a Ph.D. and taught at a university. She and he agreed they did not feel adequate to raise children of their own, and so their parental feelings were directed toward their students. She came to see me when Miss Cook died. There is a Christmas card each year. Ward so far hasn't gotten very far in politics.

13

SELF-TREATMENT

MANY PROBLEMED PEOPLE OF ALL CLASSES REFUSE TO recognize themselves as "sick" or "emotionally disturbed," and do not seek help; of these, some will spontaneously get better, some will remain the same, and some will deteriorate until some crisis forces professional intervention. Those whose problems are predominantly concerned with neurotic conflict are more likely to seek professional help. Those who suffer from dysgradia often do not recognize their empty feeling of discontent as part of an illness. They may try various maneuvers to help themselves. Mention has already been made of some of the futile and self-destructive efforts such as promiscuity and drug use. Of the more constructive efforts at self-help, some may be reasonably successful, though there may be dangers involved.

If a lack of self-esteem and a feeling of valuelessness is the problem, it certainly makes sense that one might seek out that which man has considered the most important and powerful force in the universe, God. A variety of factors determine whether one can turn to God with a sense of being saved; most crucial is the early family attitude about religion. Where the circumstances are favorable, remarkable transformations may occur. I was sitting next to a well-dressed businessman on a transcontinental flight. When the stewardess offered drinks, he refused with unusual vehemence. He sensed my curiosity about this, and before long we were talking about drinking. When he learned I was a psychiatrist he enthusiastically began telling his story.

"I used to drink a great deal—let's face it—I was an alcoholic. My wife threatened to leave me and my business career was in deep trouble. I came home very late—if at all—spending my evenings in a bar and often sleeping it off in my car."

When he mentioned his business, I recognized the name. His father had founded a major industry.

"I had everything anyone could want as a child," he continued, "born into the lap of luxury. I was a bright young whiz in college. When I went into the business I began changing. I felt empty inside and was frequently depressed.

And then the drinking started." It's not my habit to analyze casual conversations in social situations, but I couldn't help speculating that his drinking had been an effort to treat a depression, and that the depression must have been related to an inability to derive gratification from his work.

"My wife sent me to a psychiatrist—maybe you know him, Dr.———, who put me on the couch and had me babbling nonsense five days a week. I just drank more and seemed to be getting worse. He didn't even tell me to cut it out! Well, I stopped going after a few months, and tried AA. That could have helped if I could have worked up a little more enthusiasm, but I just couldn't.

"Now this will sound corny, but it's completely true: I landed in a hospital with gastritis—I was heaving blood from my alcohol-burned stomach—when I started reading the Bible. Never in my life has anything made such sense to me! Here was the actual word of God, addressed to me—it was just what I needed. I got myself baptized and began going to church. And that did it; I've never been more confident in my work—or for that matter more successful. I don't drink or smoke, but I do attend church regularly, study the Bible, and do some local missionary work. I know He saved me, and it's a tragedy that more people don't realize what He can do for them."

In place of an empty ego, devoid of any sense of purpose in life, this man is now a servant of God and has a feeling of fullness that he has never known before. This doesn't work for everyone, but when it does the results are dramatic. The gratification of feeling God inside of one becomes a satisfying way of life.

He was not fanatical, though it was important for him to

spread his discovery abroad, and find converts to religion. It's not a "treatment" most psychiatrists subscribe to, but there are times when it should be accepted and not challenged.

The sufferer from dysgradia is lucky when he can find a "cause." There is often a history of aimlessness and depression, until he hits upon his "thing." It may be a political cause, a philosophical idea, or a turning to religion. Sometimes the cause strikes us as constructive and worthwhile, sometimes as rather strange and unrealistic.

A deep devotion to a political cause or involvement with some movement or charity may fulfill the need. Marriage or attachment to a lover, often someone quite helpless who makes the dysgradia sufferer feel needed, can supply a sense of purpose, making up for the absence of a feeling of self-esteem. For the first time in his life, perhaps, he may feel gratification in the role of one person helping another. On the other hand, a love object who has a strong sense of meaningful life roles may "loan" the dysgradia sufferer the needed motivation and values to help him develop some direction to his life.

Sometimes this effort at filling the feeling of emptiness and finding a gratifying purpose in life leads one to an intriguing and potentially dangerous state of affairs: fanaticism.

The fanatic has been virtually ignored in pyschological literature. He may be an annoying kook, or, if he possesses that special quality of charisma, a very dangerous threat to society. I have encountered several true fanatics among children of the very wealthy, usually hearing about them indirectly since they seldom seek psychotherapy. Their fanatical devotion to a cause, while it lasts, lends meaning to their lives.

There are certain characteristics present in every true fanatic. First of all, there must be complete absorption in the cause, and the cause must be at some extreme end of what was once a reasonable idea. Secondly, the fanatic must be so absorbed that he can pursue his cause in complete isolation; where he has qualities of leadership he may collect a following, but that is not essential. Large numbers of people may follow extreme causes when they are supported by an approving group and strong leadership; the fanatic follows his cause whether or not he has support.

Dee was never a patient of mine. She was a close friend of one of my patients who spoke of practically nothing else for several weeks. My patient was afraid Dee would carry out her plan to blow up a major bridge. She was torn between her feeling of loyalty to her friend and her feeling that she was the only person who could prevent it.

Dee and my patient had been roommates in college. She came from a very wealthy and prominent family and had suffered from the indulged neglect which seems so common in these children. Her parents lived for long periods of time in foreign countries, and she was left to the care of servants. She grew into a beautiful girl, with sad dark eyes, and a frail helpless look. Her parents paid very little attention to her, though they were very generous financially. Dee appeared distant much of the time and kept her feelings to herself. She got along well with my patient, but was not close to anybody.

In her junior year she became involved with a small group of radical students and began showing an interest in their particular revolutionary theories. She gradually became a zealot. Her sad eyes began to blaze as she described the plans her group was hatching. She became more and more excited, until that cause seemed to become her whole existence. My patient became alarmed when Dee's group set off some explosives near government buildings, but her efforts to reason with Dee only prompted long animated lectures on her political views.

The group that Dee belonged to soon began having internal dissension and finally splintered into violently competing groups. Dee joined none of these groups; she now had a mission of her own. Over a period of a few months she had undergone a remarkable personality change. After she left the group she seemed alive and enthusiastic. It was as if for the first time in her life she had found some meaning to her existence.

I can only speculate on how this transformation took place—speculations based on closer observation of somewhat similar situations. As a result of early deprivations Dee withdrew into a shell and found herself in what is described as the "schizoid double-bind." She was starved for loving relationships and hungrily grasped at anyone who offered her some warmth. However, she could not allow herself to accept this warmth because she was literally frightened of the intensity of her longing; she feared she would devour whoever offered her love, or if she didn't she was then unbearably vulnerable to being hurt. What a terrible bind to be in: forever longing for warmth and yet fearfully avoiding it!

This situation severely impaired Dee's ability to develop a system for maintaining self-esteem. The conception of a gratifying series of life roles to progress through involves the identification with the ideals of the significant people in the immediate environment. When these people are distant or absent and care is left to servants, serious impairments develop. When there is a schizoid double-bind, the problem is greatly compounded; the people who are available as objects for identification are feared and avoided. Dee thus had virtually no sense of a gratifying series of life roles to lend meaning to her life. This would explain her sad, isolated personality. Ordinary activities were not gratifying, and ordinary relationships were too threatening. Add to this a deep reservoir of unaimed frustrated rage, and one has the makings of a fanatic.

The violent—but well-rationalized—activities would help discharge some of her anger at her family and the world. The fantasy that by some violent society-shaking act she could dramatically change the world was practically the only thing that had ever given her a feeling of importance. At last there was something that she could do that was above any need for approval. She was sure she was right and would do something of great value.

Dee had procured the explosives and knew how to use them. As the fateful day approached, my patient finally decided it was futile to reason any further with Dee. She wrote Dee's father and explained the situation. He arrived from Geneva on the day Dee was to change the world. He helped her load a panel truck full of dynamite and detonation equipment and deliver it to a startled police officer.

She cooperated completely with the authorities, was convicted of several crimes involving possession of explosives, and was allowed to avoid prison if she would seek psychiatric therapy. My knowledge of what happened after that is sketchy; she was hospitalized for a while and was said to be continuing therapy after her discharge.

Why had she gone so willingly with her father to turn herself in? I can only guess that she could not resist his demonstration of concern. Perhaps the rational part of her hoped all along he would come and save her from disaster.

Dysgradia is a painful condition. I have described some of the efforts at self-help or coping that sufferers may turn to. Probably only a relatively small percentage ever turn to psychiatrists for help; when they do, the therapist's skill and ingenuity are severely tested.

14

THE ANALYTICAL APPROACH TO TREATMENT

A WIDE VARIETY OF PROBLEMS MAY BE VIEWED AS MANI-festations of dysgradia. This defect in the normal concept of stepwise progression through life roles is by no means limited to the children of the rich. It is also the basis of many of the problems of the children of the poor, and is not unknown—though usually less extreme—in the middle classes. The emphasis here is on the treatment of those children of

THE ANALYTICAL APPROACH TO TREATMENT

the rich whose problems are severe enough that they cannot be ignored, and who do not find some form of self-treatment. Some of these, as the preceding cases illustrate, are seen by psychiatrists. Little has been written about their unique challenge to our therapeutic skills.

My general orientation toward treatment is analytical. Analytical psychotherapy—also called "dynamic psychiatry"—includes a variety of divergent approaches. There are schools of therapy modeled after the theories of certain pioneers: Freud, Jung, Adler, and a few others. There are variations on these original ideas, and a variety of "neo" groups has developed. Therapy may be individual or in a group, "deep" or "superficial," brief or extended. But among all of these therapies is far more agreement than disagreement, though the disagreements make for much more interesting discussion.

Virtually all analytical therapists emphasize the importance of early life experience in the development of problems. They may disagree as to *how* early the crucial fixations occur and whether therapy should uncover these early problems or focus on the current life derivatives. But whatever the approach, the role of heredity and chemistry is not considered the major source of the problems.

The analytical psychotherapists all utilize therapeutic techniques that recognize the existence of the unconscious and the role of unconscious conflicts and defense mechanisms in the development of problems. They all attempt to assist the patient to develop insight into the nature of his conflicts and his ways of coping with them and to effect changes in the direction of more adaptive behavior. This group of therapists recognizes that "transference phenomena" develop between patient and doctor. Reactions that once involved significant persons from the past are now seen in the interaction with the therapist. Again, the only disagreement is how crucial the development and analysis of these phenomena are to the therapeutic progress.

Once the therapist undertakes the treatment of dysgradia, he must be prepared to use considerable flexibility. The basic principles, however, remain unchanged; the individual must be understood in terms of the totality of his developmental experiences. The patient's present life situation must be seen as the result of unique childhood experiences occurring within a particular family constellation. The realities of his social milieu must be considered, along with his conception of roles within that milieu. The various developmental crises he has passed through and the ways they were resolved is also of great importance.

It would thus seem that the patient with dysgradia can be approached in the typical analytical manner. And that is true except in terms of the mechanics of the technique. These patients present problems considerably different from those that the usual analytical techniques were designed for. The overwhelming majority of patients are seen with problems—symptomatic and characterologic—that are the result of some type of internal conflict. The usual techniques involve a relatively inactive approach by the therapist whose task is to remove the various blocks—resistances—to free association. As the patient becomes freer in expressing his thoughts, feelings, and fantasies, the struggle between the conflicting trends in the personality becomes apparent.

The model for this treatment is the psychoanalytic treatment described by Sigmund Freud. The analyst was encouraged to avoid intruding his own personality into the treatment and to strive to be a "blank screen" onto which the patient can project his feelings. We know that Freud did not strictly follow his own advice, and variations were used whenever it was in his patients' best interests. However, the basic idea of this model is the most effective tool for the understanding and helping of patients in conflict.

While all analytical therapists have their own particular style of working, there is a tendency to feel vaguely uncomfortable, even guilty, when one becomes more "active." In the treatment of dysgradia one must overcome this and accept that at times the patient will need an active interchange with his doctor. While conflict is a basic quality of all human mental life, the problem of dysgradia represents a deficiency, an absence of something the personality needs; conflict may be of minor importance in the problem or may not come into focus until the dysgradia is resolved. Clearing away obstacles to free association will not correct the difficulty. Attempting to treat these patients by classical analytic techniques may produce a seriously incomplete result.

If treated by a technique utilizing free association and an inactive therapist, the patient's active conflict areas will come into focus and can be resolved. But the basic defect in identifications cannot be treated by this method. The therapist utilizing this approach is attuned to dealing only with conflict areas and their derivatives. He runs the risk of missing an important aspect of his patient's problems.

What is called for is a constant awareness on the therapist's part that he is dealing with a deficiency. If this awareness is maintained, it becomes apparent that the problem may be much more manifest in what the patient is *not* thinking and feeling, and in what does *not* happen in his life pattern and interaction with people. The absence of goals, ambitions, clearcut plans, a clear feeling of meaningful life roles—these must be the focus.

It does not matter whether the patient lies on the couch or faces the therapist. Whichever method is more comfortable for the two parties can be used. The patient is usually brought into therapy by some acute crisis. After this has been handled, the patient must be helped to recognize the defect he suffers from. It may not be apparent to him that the defect exists. He has lived with it all his life, and perhaps most of the people he has known seem just like himself. Here the therapist must actively show his patient that his personality is missing an important part. This is not as difficult to accomplish as it may sound. The patient is often relieved to understand the cause of his empty feelings and heartened at the prospect of developing a greater purpose for living.

My more recent thinking concerning the technique of working with these patients is illustrated by the treatment of Ivan.

15

IVAN: THE CRISIS

THE PATIENT WITH DYSGRADIA USUALLY ENTERS THERapy because of some type of crisis. Thus the first task is to help resolve the acute problem. The approach, of course, depends on the nature of the problem and may be handled in the office or require hospitalization. This period may require only a few weeks for resolution or, in the case of a serious personality disruption, occupy many months. But usually the acute crisis is much more easily treated than the more basic problem of dysgradia. This was certainly the case with Ivan.

Ivan was the son of the owner of a fleet of oil tankers. When he was twenty-one years old he received control of a trust fund worth many millions of dollars. He left college, which he was attending at the insistence of his parents, and began an aimless, pleasure-oriented life. He maintained a lavish Sunset Strip apartment and had innumerable affairs. He attempted producing a movie, but that undertaking was a disaster. He drank a great deal, sniffed some cocaine, and gave large parties almost nightly. He probably never would have seen a psychiatrist had he not taken up flying.

When he was thirty-two, he rather impulsively bought an airplane. He then started flying lessons. After a few hours of instruction he took a girl friend out for an unauthorized midnight flight. They were both moderately high on drugs. After flying over the desert for several pleasant hours he headed back to Los Angeles. To his horror, as they approached the city he discovered a thick layer of fog had rolled in.

Ivan began to panic. He did not know the landmarks well enough to find an alternate field. He desperately attempted to get help by radio but had failed to switch it on and concluded that it was broken. He began laughing uncontrollably and his girl friend began screaming. He decided to set down in the first open field he saw—through sheer luck a fairly level golf course. The approach was too fast and too steep, and the landing gear gave way. The plane ended up nose down in a sand trap, a total loss. Except for bruises, Ivan and the girl were unhurt.

IVAN: THE CRISIS

A few days later his lawyer, Mr. Narahara, called me. Since the accident, Ivan had developed some severe symptoms. He was afraid of being alone and his lawyer had taken him to stay with him and his wife. Ivan would not drive a car and became moderately anxious when driven by somebody else. He could not ride on the freeways. He was sleeping very poorly and awakening frequently during the night reliving the terror of the plane crash. He would have periods of uncontrollable laughter.

Mr. Narahara had taken care of Ivan's legal affairs over the years and was genuinely concerned about the direction his life was heading. He knew of the drug use and had made several unsuccessful efforts to interest Ivan in psychotherapy. Now he felt the accident might be a blessing in disguise, a chance to get him the help he needed. Ivan readily agreed to see me.

He appeared for his appointment wearing pajamas and a bathrobe. He was tall, thin, and tanned, with handsome angular features. He was wide-eyed and tremulous. His voice was strained and it was obvious that he was extremely anxious. My impression was that he was suffering from a traumatic neurosis—a state of shock resulting from an overwhelming flood of anxiety that the person feels helpless to control in any way. In 1918 it would have been called "shell shock."

So now this young man, presenting a typical picture of dysgradia, had encountered a series of events that brought him into therapy. I knew the acute crisis would respond fairly quickly to therapy and that the difficult period was to come later. The major task now was to help him to go over and over what had happened while he experienced the anxiety in doses small enough to master. By initiating treatment immediately and intensively, a chronic state of anxiety could be avoided.

A week later he was able to drive himself to his appointments. He was neatly dressed, but still appeared quite anxious. I asked, "How are you feeling today?"

"Each day seems a little better. I only woke up once last night."

"A dream?"

"Yes, the same one. We're going to crash and my heart was pounding so hard that I was sure I was going to have a heart attack when I woke up. Only this time I remembered something more. The girl I was with was screaming her lungs out! I remember trying to remember what my instructor had said about the approach, but all that my brain could register was her shrill screams—over and over."

His forehead was wet with perspiration and his pupils were dilated. He got up and walked around the room for a few minutes before he could sit down and continue.

This therapeutic approach continued for about a month. I felt it would be a mistake to give him tranquilizers or sleeping pills. He simply had to master the experience he had been through. Drugs would only have prolonged the process. The anxiety gradually subsided and he began sleeping through the night. His phobia about automobiles also disappeared. It became apparent that the feelings of movement he experienced in a car—particularly the sensations of acceleration and deceleration—had reminded him of the helpless terror in the airplane immediately before the crash. As his anxiety subsided he was able to move back to his apartment and resume his more normal activities.

The character of the hours began to change. He no longer came in eagerly, seeking relief from his suffering. The reluctance to leave when our time was up was diminishing. Whereas the hours had been filled with his talking about how he was feeling, his dreams, and the memories of the accident, long pauses now appeared during which he seemed unsure what to say.

I also noticed a change in how I felt during the hours. I would find my attention wandering and noticed that the hours seemed longer. The acute problem had been resolved. We were now at a crucial juncture; either the therapy would be terminated, or we would proceed to the treatment of his dysgradia.

It was up to me to clarify what was happening. "Ivan, the acute symptoms that brought you into therapy have pretty much subsided."

"Amen! This has been some experience. I appreciate what you've done for me."

"We have to decide where we go from here. We could stop meeting fairly soon, or we can continue with your therapy. There are serious problems we haven't touched on yet."

Ivan grinned. "Narahara's been talking to you. That old Jap's been after me to see a psychiatrist for years. I think he was tickled I damn near creamed myself so he could get me in here. OK—what about my head needs adjusting?"

"Finding that out is a big part of the therapy. Are you willing to go on?"

Ivan paused. The flippancy which had been developing as he began feeling better left him for a moment. "Yes, I know there's something wrong with my life. I do pointless things and have been getting into drugs. But I'm not really *that* screwed up. Before that damn plane incident there wasn't anything too seriously wrong with me . . ."

"That might depend on one's point of view. How contented have you been with your life?"

"I don't know. I never have thought much about it. I've had lots of fun and had a lot of wild experiences."

The analyst can't be passive with the COR. There isn't enough internal conflict to motivate him to pursue therapy. With the more typical patient there would be no need to convince him of his need for help. I had to force Ivan to begin evaluating how he felt about himself and what he thought about his life. I could do this now because he trusted me and had some positive feelings toward me. Unless I could arouse some awareness in him that his pleasure-oriented, impulsive way of life was to cover up a painful emptiness, there would never be any hope for change.

"OK, you've had some wild experiences—like landing a forty-thousand-dollar plane in a sand trap. But you're not answering me: How do you feel about your life?"

Ivan looked blank. He wasn't used to having people give him orders, and I was making a demand that he look inside and answer my question.

"It doesn't make much sense, I guess," he answered. "My doctor says I can get into real trouble with the cocaine, but I don't seem to give a damn. There's something wrong with that. And I have lots of dates, but don't care enough about any of them to get serious."

I felt I had to press the point. "What else?"

Again, a puzzled thoughtfulness. "Well sometimes I just stay in bed all day and sniff cocaine. I daydream about doing really hot-shot things . . . being like Howard Hughes, maybe. . . ."

I told him I thought he used the cocaine to keep from feeling really bad about himself.

"I guess I don't really like not having anything to do," he said. "That's probably why I tried producing that movie. . . . Boy did I get taken! But it was sort of fun for a while."

An acute crisis had brought a COR into therapy. Without some such crisis he would probably never have seen a psychiatrist. The acute crisis had been resolved, and he was just barely becoming aware that he had been living with a serious problem. Now the therapy of dysgradia was beginning.

16

IVAN: ATTACKING DYSGRADIA

It has been stressed that dysgradia is not a specific form of emotional problem; rather, it is a defect in the individual's personality structure. This defect involves the inadequate development of role images that enable the person to maintain his self-esteem. Now that the acute problem which had brought Ivan into therapy was resolved, the next task was to make him aware of this defect.

IVAN: ATTACKING DYSGRADIA

What purpose would be served by making an individual aware of a handicap? In answering that question one must realize the tremendous capacity for adaptation that people are capable of. The blind can become remarkably self-sufficient, amputees can learn to function as well as those with all their limbs intact. But it is obvious that these accomplishments take considerable time and effort. And it is also obvious that the overcoming of a handicap would be impossible if the individual did not realize he had that problem. This was the situation with Ivan at the beginning of this second phase of treatment.

The capacity for psychological adaptation is every bit as great as the capacity to adapt to physical defects. But Ivan was largely unaware that he had a problem. This was not the place for a passive approach to therapy. The nature of his handicap had to be brought home to him. This period of therapy called for an active role on the part of the therapist to help Ivan realize what he lacked.

In any therapeutic undertaking that aims at the gaining of insight, one relies on an alliance with a portion of the patient's personality. A part of our mental apparatus is always standing aside observing our own behavior. It is there even when we are living out the most neurotic aspects of our personality. It is called the observing ego. In therapy the analyst and this observing ego have entered into an agreement to work together to constructively observe and evaluate what the rest of the personality is doing. In the treatment of the more typical neurotic problems this liaison is taken for granted. In dysgradia, the powers of the observing ego must be awakened and directed.

Ivan arrived a few minutes late for an afternoon hour at

the beginning of the fifth month of therapy. His observing ego anticipated my question. "OK, you want me to explore whether there is some psychological reason for being late. Well, I'll tell you why I'm late. I was so goddamned hung over I could hardly get out of bed. It's a tribute to my loyalty to you that I'm here altogether."

He really didn't look unwell. He was clean-shaven and neatly dressed, and his eyes were clear. "You had a party last night?"

"I guess you could call it that. Ten or so people from my building came up and we whooped it up."

"You don't look that hung over. Is something else bothering you?" I asked.

"I don't know what you mean, Doc. I had a party, drank too much, and now I feel crummy."

"Examine how you're feeling now."

Ivan's face became a bit flushed. "Well right now I'm feeling a little pissed-off with you. But besides that I was feeling sort of depressed as I was driving over here. I assumed it was just from the party."

I asked, "Is there anything about last night that you would feel depressed about?"

Ivan flushed again. "You don't give up, do you? Well, I did feel sort of crummy about one thing. I really didn't particularly feel like having that bunch up to my place last night. We were sitting around the pool and someone said, 'Let's go up to Ivan's pad,' and pretty soon we're having a party. I've always invited them, so they just sort of assume it's always open house."

He was looking somewhat perplexed. I noticed a slight degree of wheezing was beginning.

"Well I guess I really was feeling resentful, and I started sort of watching everybody. And I started thinking that I really didn't like anybody there. And for a moment I felt like crying. You know, this analysis is ruining my social life."

"Why did you have them up when you didn't really feel like it?" I asked.

"You want me to say I need to keep running to avoid realizing how empty I feel."

"I don't want you to say anything except what you're feeling."

"Well I guess that's it. That feeling of wanting to cry—that's the emptiness you're talking about. . . ."

This kind of active interchange went on for months. Ivan was a very easygoing young man, accustomed to having his comforts and not thinking very much about his feelings or those of others. But he had a surprising capacity for introspection; sometimes I wondered why I didn't have to work harder. Aside from the aimless, self-indulgent, and somewhat impulsive life-style, there was not really very much that one could call abnormal about what he did. The abnormality was in what he did not do: there was virtually nothing that Ivan did about which he felt any gratification.

These hours of actively challenging him to examine his feelings went on for most of the first year of therapy. Inevitably his feelings led him to the awareness that he was unhappy with his way of life. I put into words for him the fact that there was nothing that he did about which he could take pride. He was gaining insight into the nature of his handicap and an awareness of the underlying feelings of emptiness and sadness.

These hours were not particularly pleasant ones for me. The exciting discoveries of dream analysis, the satisfying feeling of empathy in helping a patient resolve a difficult conflict, the challenge to one's therapeutic skills when a patient is reliving a crucial childhood event in the transference—none of these was present. Hour after hour of actively confronting and challenging Ivan eventually became monotonous and often boring. I began to wonder whether we were getting anyplace, whether this investment in time and energy would prove worthwhile.

Gradually, a subtle change became apparent. I became aware that the feelings of boredom were decreasing and that I was feeling more positive toward him. That touch of sadness which had first begun to appear many hours before was now quite pronounced. I was talking less and listening more. My awareness that Ivan had never developed a satisfactory method for maintaining his self-esteem was now his awareness too. Instead of a self-indulgent playboy, he was now a man aware of a serious problem.

Now that he was aware of his handicap, his efforts at finding some solution to his problem became apparent. His way of life changed. He no longer used drugs and he drank very little. He had some friends over occasionally for dinner, but there were no more noisy parties. He felt sad a great deal of the time, but he did not seem to mind it. He liked being alone and feeling sad. He would say it was like renewing an old friendship.

My role was fairly clear during the preceding period of Ivan's therapy—I had to actively confront him with his dysgradia. Now the nature of the therapy was shifting. I no longer felt that I was ahead of him; I said very little and was following with interest where he was leading us. I felt some uneasiness about his interest in being alone and contemplating this expanding feeling of sadness, but my intuition told me to follow along with him without interfering.

Well into the second year of therapy he had changed quite a bit. He had lost some weight and seemed quieter. He went out very little though he did date occasionally. He presented a thoughtful, serious manner which contrasted strikingly with the flippant attitude during the early period of therapy. He was very much involved in his therapy, and at his request I was seeing him five times a week. He asked if he could lie on the couch, he felt he could follow his thoughts better, and I had no objection.

Confronting him with the nature of the life he was leading had enabled him to evaluate it with his observing ego. His response was that he did not like it, and quite dramatically he repudiated it. It had served to ward off the unpleasant feelings that resulted from the defect in his ability to derive gratification from his life. He chose to examine those feelings and remain in a more or less constant state of suffering.

Now in pursuing his therapy he had learned a method for deriving gratification from his efforts. Even while he was suffering, he recognized he was involved in a difficult, challenging, and exciting undertaking. He now had a goal—to follow his feelings and find out as much as he could about himself. I wondered briefly if he was building his therapy into another self-indulgent escape from the challenges of the external world, but I decided that this was a serious and meaningful quest he was on. His life had changed quite a bit. He read a great deal, had begun collecting some rare books about boats, and was taking an active part in the managing of his finances. Dysgradia was disappearing as a problem, and the therapy had shifted to a more conventional analysis of the personality.

17

IVAN:
THE ANALYSIS

TOWARD THE END OF THE SECOND YEAR OF THERAPY Ivan reported an unusual occurrence. "Last night after I got in bed I remembered the boat we had when I was four or five. It was a small sloop that Dad used to sail on the lake near our summer cottage. I could see Dad in the boat with his arms out for me. I think I was frightened and cried as he lifted me aboard. And then that feeling of sadness came over me, and it felt as if I was missing somebody. There was a real sense of loss. And then I cried for a few seconds, and then I got short of breath. Then I fell asleep."

His thoughts led to memories of his father who had died when Ivan was twenty-five. He had always felt good when he was with his father, though he could remember seeing relatively little of him during his childhood.

"Father traveled a great deal attending to business. I can't remember much about Mother. You know she didn't attend much to me—left me mostly to the servants."

Mother was then in her seventies and still very active in civic affairs. There had been no closeness between them during his childhood, and she had had nothing to do with him after he left college against her wishes. Now they were on a friendly basis, and he took her out to dinner occasionally. There was also a sister nine years older than he; they had little contact as he was growing up, and he saw her only a few times a year. His thoughts about Father's traveling and Mother's absence from his memories led to thoughts about the servants who took care of him.

"I remember two different ones—Martha and Jan. Martha was there till I was around four, and then Jan came. I'd forgotten about Martha. She was Mexican, I think, and pretty and young. She used to sing to me and read to me." He was silent a few moments. "I seem blocked," he said.

"Something about Martha?" I asked. I noted that he was wheezing.

"Yes—the old sadness seemed to well up as I thought about her, and then it suddenly shut off."

He looked pale and tired when he arrived for his hour the next day. "You almost got called at 2 A.M. I'd been reading late, and when I got into bed I had that feeling of crying for a second. Then I got short of breath and felt a little panicky. I started to call you—figured I was having some sort of anxiety attack—but then I realized I was wheezing and my chest felt like it was filling up with mucus. I called my internist and he told me to meet him at the UCLA Hospital Emergency Room.

"I got dressed, but by then it was pretty bad. I was actually gasping for breath. I called the fire department and they came right over and gave me oxygen. When I wasn't at UCLA, my doctor called my apartment and came right over. He gave me some injections and I started feeling better in about ten minutes. He was going to hospitalize me, but it kept getting better, and in about forty-five minutes it was almost all gone."

I asked what he thought had caused it.

"My internist said it must have been allergic asthma from something I'd eaten or breathed in. But I don't think that's it. It had something to do with the sadness."

I said, "Ivan, there is a connection between a suppressed urge to cry and asthma attacks. After you stopped running you became aware of that deep feeling of sadness. Recently it seems as if you want to cry but something shuts it off. I think that's what caused the asthma."

During the next five months there were frequent episodes of asthma. He was able to relieve them by using an inhaler when the wheezing first started. He pursued his therapy with great energy—determined to unravel the connection between his sadness, the urge to cry, and the asthma. And how these related to himself as an individual.

"You know, I feel you think I'm a little hung up on this

sadness business. But I feel that I need to put that together before I can start being a person. I'm not a bum anymore, and I have real friends and do things I can take pride in. But I still don't feel all together. It's like I'm not complete, a puzzle with an important piece missing.

"It's hard to describe. I feel as if I carry something heavy around all the time. Anyway, I've got to figure it out to get rid of this asthma. I'm using the adrenalin spray two or three times a week now."

Over and over during this period we had seen how the asthma would appear just as his feeling of sadness progressed to a few sobs. The sobs would be abruptly squeezed off and some mild wheezing would appear during the hours. While this happened occasionally when he was home, it was mostly limited to his hours. He would feel the process begin as he approached my waiting room, and it was practically gone soon after he left.

During these months I pointed out to him many times how he seemed to be fighting the urge to cry, and how the asthma seemed to be the result of suppressing the tears. He understood, but seemed unable to release the emotion. I began to feel he was becoming too dependent on the asthma medication. The sadness and urge to cry must be related to some deep emotional loss. Perhaps the inhaler he carried around in his pocket was becoming a symbol of security, like a child's favorite blanket or Teddy bear. I suggested he try to cut down on its use and save it only for severe asthma.

The suggestion increased his feelings of sadness, and his dreams and associations kept leading to himself as an unhappy little boy. References to Martha came up again and again. He reconstructed the world he lived in in his first four years. There were no other children. His sister attended a private school and was home only occasionally. She wasn't much interested in him when she was there. His mother was home most of the time, but she traveled sometimes with Father. She was completely wrapped up in club work and left his care almost completely to the servants. With some bitterness he realized how cold and unloving she had been.

His father was warm toward him, and there were memories of laughter and happy play together. "But he sure didn't stay home much. I think maybe he couldn't stand Mother. There's a memory of one terrible fight between them. I must have been around four. Maybe it was about his traveling—maybe Mother objected. But he was warm and affectionate—how could he stay home with that ice cube? But I suffered—I really needed him. . . ."

Ivan was crying. He had often felt sad, and he had shed a few tears on occasion. But now he was crying freely, with tears streaming down his face and deep sobbing. As he released this pent-up emotion, I, too, felt a tremendous sense of relief.

Through a massive effort at repression these tears had been bottled up since he was a young child. As the repression began to lift, the asthma had appeared. The unconscious fights a last-ditch stand against revealing its secrets. As repression gave way, a psychosomatic symptom appeared. The tears could be hidden awhile longer by a complicated process in which nerve impulses are shunted from the tear glands to the lungs. But now that defense against emotion had been resolved.

For the greater part of seven months Ivan cried. The tears would start flowing as soon as he lay down on the couch.

Sometimes he could not speak at all during the hour. He cried for Martha and for his father. The picture of his early years became clear. He had deeply loved Martha who had been with him from birth.

"She was so sweet and warm," he sobbed. "It seems as if I was with her constantly. I remember her holding me while I explored her face. I would pull her nose and her hair—she just smiled and let me. Then we'd go for walks around the gardens—we'd spend hours looking at the flowers, watching the clouds and the birds . . ."

He recalled that there had also been considerable contact with Father during that period. They would play together a little every day, and he sometimes went riding in the car with him. "Those were happy years," he recalled. "The crying goes back to a later period."

When he was about three and a half, Martha left to get married. He recalled missing her a great deal, but it seemed as if he became closer to Father for a while.

"After she left I spent more time with Dad. I shifted my attachment from Martha to him. Then it seems that something happened—the happy times with him rather suddenly disappear from my memories when I'm about four. Maybe something changed in his business, and he had to be gone more."

Ivan asked his mother if something had happened when he was about four. She told him that Father began an affair with the wife of a business associate which lasted for about eight years. From that point on it was a marriage in appearance only—he was away most of the time.

The picture of these early years was now fairly clear, as was the source of the sadness and tears. His first few years

IVAN: THE ANALYSIS

were fairly typical of so many children of the rich. He was largely ignored by his mother and his care was turned over to servants. There were no other children for him to share experiences with. He was fortunate in that he had a father who was warm and cared about him, and that he had Martha to care for him.

The contact with Martha during those crucial first three and a half years had been tremendously important for the development of his basic personality. She had given him a sense of security and a love of life that had sustained him during the difficult, unhappy years which followed. From her he learned sensitivity, curiosity, and a quiet patience. This explained the surprising degree of sensitivity and patience he had shown in his analysis. I had often wondered how he managed to pursue his analysis in spite of considerable emotional and physical suffering without ever complaining. Now it was clear; he had a strong identification with this warm, tolerant woman who had loved him so much as a child.

After Martha left he turned to his father to make up for the loss. For a few months he managed to maintain an equilibrium; it appears that Father did respond fairly well to the needs of his son. But when Ivan was four, Father's other involvement took him away, and he was left with nobody he felt close to. Martha's replacement, Jan, was efficient but cold. With the loss of Martha, and then Father, Ivan's world collapsed. The tears went back to that point in his life. In his thirties he was reliving the grief that had not been expressed when he was four.

Why had it been buried so long? What had stopped the four-year-old from going through a period of grief and mourning for his losses? Ivan and I reconstructed a set of circumstances that seemed to fit the facts and explain the situation. The memory of his father lifting him into the boat took on new significance.

"I remembered more about it yesterday when I was having dinner with Mother," he said. He was now in the fourth year of his treatment, and there was a feeling that we were nearing the end of our work. "After Dad began staying away so much, I would cry whenever he came home to see me. I guess seeing him reminded me how unhappy and lonely I was. I remember more about his lifting me into that boat. I was crying—guess I'd never been in a boat before. Father lifted me in and set me down next to him."

Ivan was crying now as he relived this memory. "He looked angry at me—that's the only time in my whole life that I can remember that look on his face. He said, 'Men don't cry, and you mustn't cry. You must be strong and brave and not act like a baby.' I stopped crying and we had a great time. That probably has something to do with my love of boats.

"I needed him so much, and there was so little of him. I'd do anything in the world to please him. It may seem a little pat, but I think I decided right then and there that I'd never cry anymore. Mother told me that I had some asthma for a few years from about four to six."

Ivan's life during the years that followed was typical of so many unfortunate CORs. He saw little of his parents and sister and had no children to play with. He was cared for by a series of efficient but relatively unconcerned servants. He was unhappy, but repressed those feelings—perhaps out of a need to be strong like his father.

The need for his father led Ivan to fantasize a great deal

about him. He imagined him traveling around the world on important business missions. As he grew older he imagined Father as a race car driver and would invent exciting races in which Father triumphed in fierce competition. There was so little contact with real people to identify with that he had to invent this idealized superfather.

This identification explained many of the characteristics of the years before Ivan entered therapy. He was still searching for the idealized father. His incessant pursuit of new women and the recklessness about his personal well-being—notably his experience as a pilot—were efforts to live up to an image of a strong father which he had created as a child. The rather flippant way he reacted to me early in the therapy was both a childlike effort to convey an air of masculinity and a denial of his longing for a father.

The fantasy of the idealized father could not sustain him. The pointlessness of his life as a playboy was apparent to him and he gradually gave it up. What was underneath was a terrible absence of identifications that could supply him with gratifying goals and aspirations. Analysis supplied him with an accepting person he could depend on. In the transference, I represented Martha to him for much of the analysis. That explained the unquestioning trust and the minimal amount of competitiveness. I was also a real person to him; a man who cared about him, accepted his feelings, and whom he did not have to idealize. There was enough of me as a real person for him to form some degree of identification with.

Gradually the crying stopped. Mourning runs a course and ends. Ivan gradually needed me and analysis less and less. He was now a more complete person; out of his reawakened identification with Martha, his realistic perception of his father, and his long contact with me, he developed his own unique sense of identity. He evolved as a quiet, thoughtful, sensitive man, rather distant from most people, but capable of great loyalty and warmth.

Ivan's life was now quite full and gratifying. He was seriously involved with a schoolteacher whom he later married. He sailed for recreation and had acquired a large collection of books about boats. He was active in various business projects. He had become a director of the family's charitable foundation and was involved in evaluating requests for research grants. This latter activity gave him a great deal of satisfaction.

Near the end of the fourth year of treatment, we decided to terminate at the end of that year. It was a difficult few months for both of us. It was difficult for me to believe that this substantial man had been the flippant brat whom Mr. Narahara had brought to my office. I had strong fatherly feelings toward him now and had to work through my own feelings of satisfaction and sadness about the termination.

Ivan's feelings were similar. The approaching termination reactivated the old feelings of loss from his childhood, and he had a brief recurrence of asthma and then crying. His separating from me enabled him to work through the remnants of his childhood problems. Ivan and I both felt a little tearful as we shook hands at the end of his last hour.

18

COUNTERTRANSFERENCE

COUNTERTRANSFERENCE REFERS HERE TO ANY REACTION on the part of the therapist that interferes with his effective treatment of a patient. Since most analysts have middle-class origins, they can usually empathize with the basic values of their middle-class patients. The countertransference problems which arise are likely to involve residuals of the analyst's own areas of conflict. An example might be a delay in detecting a patient's emerging hostility toward father figures because the patient is reactivating some old, similar problem in the analyst. Such situations are usually easily resolved; analysts constantly watch for indications that such problems are developing in themselves.

The therapist treating a COR must be aware of the differences between his middle-class values and the values of his patient. There is a tendency to be critical of the COR's lack of life direction, and to react to it as if it were a sign of laziness and moral decay. The therapist must be aware that his middle-class values are adaptive for his own life situation but cannot be applied to the COR's. Once the therapist recognizes this, he can begin to empathize more closely with the kind of life situation the COR was raised in and lives in. It may be startlingly different from his own.

One set of the analyst's biases may be offered to the patient: that life should have some purpose, that man must have some set of goals or aspirations and that, hopefully, these contribute something constructive to the world. The therapist must be willing to accept that this last point might have to be compromised to the extent that a life-style might be satisfactory as long as no one is harmed by it.

Envy is a basic human tendency, and the psychotherapist is not immune. Whether or not it interferes with therapy is dependent on the therapist's ability to deal with it. The need to be able to constantly self-analyze one's own reactions to patients is one reason that all psychotherapists must undergo thorough analyses themselves. There is a tendency to envy the wealth of the CORs; the therapist must recognize this when it arises in himself, and be alert to any tendencies this envy may have to interfere with the treatment.

In addition to his own envy and his tendency to judge others by his middle-class values, there is another factor that may make treatment ineffective. This is the tendency to assume that what we know about middle-class patients applies to all patients. What is true for our usual patients may not at all apply to those from other groups.

When the tools we are accustomed to using do not work effectively, one tendency we have is to conclude we have not used them properly or forcefully enough. The idea that we are using the wrong tools may be slow in developing. I once treated a patient who, prior to moving to California, had been in treatment with an analyst in New York. The patient had been seen four times a week in conventional psychoanalysis for several years.

In my work with this patient it became apparent that he had not benefited particularly from this treatment. He was repeatedly told by his analyst that he was resisting, that he was deeply repressing his sexual conflicts. The patient was lonely and desperately in need of help. He brought in dreams and other material that he hoped would please his analyst but it never did. He entered therapy with me convinced that he was a very bad patient who had failed in his previous treatment.

The fact was that this patient had little conflict concerning his aggressive and sexual drives. He suffered from more or less uncomplicated dysgradia. The tools of psychoanalysis, so effective when we are dealing with neurosis, were simply not able to help this patient. He did benefit over the next several years from the more active, more flexible kind of treatment I have previously described.

At a psychiatric meeting I met this patient's former analyst. He was aware that his treatment had not particularly helped the patient and tended to blame himself. He said, "You know, if I had it to do over, I would completely change my approach. Instead of seeing him four times a week I would insist he come in five times. And instead of allowing him to take two-month vacations to Europe every summer, I would insist he limit his vacation to the two or three weeks I take. I was just too easygoing with him!" If a tool proves inadequate for doing a job, then use it more vigorously!

Countertransference usually refers to problems arising in the therapy due to the therapist's own conflict areas. If the problem is due to the therapist's lack of knowledge concerning a particular kind of problem, then there is the question of whether that should be called a countertransference difficulty. I think so; if the therapist is unable to recognize and accept the fact that he is not helping a patient, then he is revealing some evidence of unresolved conflict in himself. This may involve an unconscious fantasy of omnipotence, perhaps covering up old inferiority feelings. Whatever it is due to, this kind of rigidity is harmful to the patient.

One problem concerning the treatment of CORs involves the fee. How much should one charge per hour when dealing with people of virtually unlimited resources? There is the aphorism in psychoanalysis that the treatment will be meaningful only when it involves a sacrifice on the part of the patient. For some of the CORs, thousands of dollars an hour would not be a real sacrifice. Such extremely high fees would surely be damaging to therapy.

On the part of the patient, he would be aware that any extremely high fee was making him one of the therapist's special patients. Since there is already a tendency to see the therapist in a servant role, the high fee would make him feel that he had bought the therapist and could make whatever demands he wished. While this could be dealt with in the therapy, there might always be a lingering feeling in the patient that he was being exploited, and consequently a distrust of the therapist's good intentions.

An extremely high fee is also harmful in terms of its effect on the therapist. A high fee is perhaps one reason why a therapist would not easily recognize that he was not helping a patient. The awareness that one patient is contributing more to one's income than any other could insidiously introduce bias into the treatment. The wish to keep the patient in treatment would be understandable, but could unconsciously induce the therapist to avoid necessary confrontations that might upset the relationship.

When I first went into practice I received a phone call from a young woman.

"Is this Dr. Wixen?"

"Yes."

"Well, my name is Marilyn Young and I'd like to start seeing you for analysis."

When one first sets out in practice all referrals are especially appreciated, and if one is in training to become a psychoanalyst, a patient wanting psychoanalysis is like a gift of the gods.

"Who suggested you call me?" I asked, wondering who my benefactor was.

"I got your name from the telephone book."

That was jarring; maybe she thought all therapy—even once a week—was psychoanalysis. Maybe she was an impulsive character who would quickly leave therapy for some new impulsive idea. Maybe—but I decided to make an appointment and evaluate the situation.

A rather pretty young woman appeared, dressed in paint-splattered jeans.

"You got my name from the telephone book?" I asked.

"Yes. I know that's a lousy way to find an analyst but I just moved to Los Angeles and I don't know anyone. Anyway, I have a friend in analysis, and she told me you can't go wrong if he's a real M.D."

Her naïveté was beginning to upset me a bit. "There are lots of psychiatrists in the phone book—how did you pick Wixen?"

She answered, "My name is Young and I've always been at the end of lists. So I always start at the end of lists and work backward. You were the first psychiatrist I came to whose office was close to me."

I would have preferred it if her call had been the result of a vote of confidence from a senior colleague. At any rate she described certain anxiety symptoms and mild phobias and it seemed she was a good candidate for psychoanalysis. I asked her what she knew about that form of treatment.

"Oh, I'll come four times a week, and lie on the couch, and say whatever comes into my mind. My friend told me all about it."

"Are you financially able to undertake this?" I asked, noting a patch in her jeans.

"Oh yes! Grandpa left me a trust fund, and you just send your bill to the bank and they pay you. What's your fee?"

I told her the prevailing fee at that time was twenty dollars an hour.

"My friend pays seventy-five dollars an hour. Why don't

you bill the bank for that? They have millions to spend on me."

My head was spinning. When she left I started calculating how much I would be earning if I saw her four times a week. Why not five times? Times eleven months a year. ... I immediately called a senior analyst for a consultation. Part of one's training in psychoanalysis involves weekly supervision of at least three cases, and I was anxious to know whether my prospective supervisor agreed that she was a suitable case. I also felt I needed some immediate help with the fee problem.

My supervisor agreed she would be an excellent case. He also agreed that I had a real problem about the fee. He felt I had to resolve my feelings about it before the treatment could get underway. That was no easy matter. In my own training analysis I spoke about my excitement with this patient and about the importance of the money to me. I was preoccupied with greedy fantasies. It became clear that I simply could not charge that amount and treat her effectively.

When I saw her again, I told her that the fee would be lower, and I set it just a bit above the standard fee. Through my training analysis and my case supervision, that "extra bit" was enough of a problem to enable me to gain considerable insight into my own feelings about money and the effects it has on the course of treatment. Her analysis was quite successful.

The experience left me convinced that one must decide what his maximum, minimum, and standard fees are. The maximum fee must be one that the therapist feels he can accept without excessive conflict. In spite of a very careful psychoanalysis, the therapist from a middle-class background can never be completely freed of his conflicts about money. An excessively high fee will be disruptive to therapy. This may become one of the major stumbling blocks in the treatment of the rich. And under the best of circumstances the treatment is difficult.

19
A SUITE
AT THE TOP
WITH INSURANCE

IN THIS AND THE NEXT FEW CHAPTERS I WILL DESCRIBE some ideas I have had for helping CORs. They may or may not work out, but might be worth trying. These thoughts apply to those who are not motivated for, or capable of, the prolonged therapy that was described in the case of Ivan.

If one looks beyond the therapist-patient relationship at what resources might be available for helping the patient, one is often struck by the plethora of riches around him. While his life might be empty and impoverished, he is certainly not lacking in wealth or social contacts. Why not put these resources to use?

When one is attempting to help the patient reach meaningful commitments for his life, why not explore with him those he knows whose life patterns he admires? Suppose he has some interest in business activities, but has no real need for subjecting himself to any prolonged period of work and sacrifice to reach some goal. Why not use his riches to step directly into that goal? Our hypothetical subject has been well educated, is socially very poised, and is not particularly bound up with neurotic anxieties. He has spent his whole life with wealthy and powerful people and is probably strongly identified with them—for what they are rather than the idea of how they got there. In short, he ought to be ideal in an executive position, though he lacks the usual incentives for getting there.

Perhaps he could contact some admired family friend and enlist his help. The therapist, patient, and friend might meet together to map out the plan. Once he understood the problem and his cooperation was enlisted, resources could potentially be made available which are far beyond the reach of most people.

If a particular type of industry was found which the patient decided he wanted to involve himself in, the best expert advice could be obtained to locate—or create—a position. Purchasing an entire business or a significant block of stock in an industry might be easily accomplished. With the help of the family resources, the patient might quickly be involved in a profitable and powerful position. The gratification would

A SUITE AT THE TOP WITH INSURANCE

surely be there, and though the tools for getting there on his own were lacking, he has many of the attributes for successfully carrying out his new position.

But there is of course the possibility that this endeavor could be a costly fiasco. Our hypothetical patient certainly does not have the years of background in business to cope with the subtleties of his new position. Economic changes or labor problems could easily wipe him out. Are we not talking about simply buying a very costly new toy for our spoiled patient?

Not necessarily. We are assuming that our hypothetical patient has had enough therapy to be aware of the nature of his problem. We are assuming that his chosen area of involvement was not capriciously decided upon, and we are assuming that certain basic personality traits indicate an aptitude for that position. Furthermore we are assuming that the best available expert assistance has been obtained and that the plan has been exhaustively researched before being put into effect. We can even go one step further, considering the resources which are available, and buy "insurance."

Our hypothetical patient, stepping into his new position, is able to purchase insurance in terms of hiring a comprehensive and competent staff of helpers. He could hire those with outstanding experience in any field. He could have a backup staff ready to step in should it develop that there was a miscalculation in preparing the plan. Enough such insurance could be purchased to make the risks acceptable.

What a tremendous investment to get one rich kid to work! What else has he to do with his money? And more important, what else has he to do with his life? The capital would be left to grow and would probably never be of any benefit to anyone. This plan would at least get one person to lead a more useful life—after all, high level executives are necessary for the running of our society. And perhaps this experience in using capital in an imaginative manner to create a more meaningful life might inspire our patient to more ambitious goals—even possibly to helping others.

There is a precedent for this kind of jump to the top. The very highest offices of government are often successfully filled by people who have never had any experience directly related to their office. A war hero may become President on the basis of his popularity and the public's confidence that he will know how to assemble a capable staff of advisors. Ambassadors and all levels of political appointees are often from wealthy classes and without special qualification for their particular assignments. And aside from the question of whether it ought to be that way, they often do very capable jobs.

I do not know of any cases in which this exact approach has been tried. The nearest thing to it involved a young man I saw a few years ago. He was sent to me by his parents who were disgusted with his aimless way of life. He, too, was rather unhappy with it, but managed to keep himself constantly diverted with travels all over the earth. The damage done by the indulged neglect of his childhood was quite severe. He had little motivation for change, and there was not very much capacity for introspection.

During the few visits we had, he discussed his unhappiness with his life-style. His one great pleasure involved exploring far-off lands. I half-kiddingly suggested he ought to own a travel agency. He jumped at that idea. It would give him something to be occupied with when he was in town, it

A SUITE AT THE TOP WITH INSURANCE

would satisfy his parents' wish for him to do some kind of work, and it would enable him to continue his travels whenever he wished.

He opened a travel agency in a large new office building and hired a manager with considerable experience in the business. The enterprise earned a profit the first year. He is not deeply committed to it, but it has produced a favorable shift in his life. He is able to use his considerable experience to help his clients plan their travels. He apparently does a good job and derives considerable gratification from it.

This modest experience with a COR using his wealth to make a more meaningful life for himself suggests that a more ambitious effort in this direction might be fruitful.

20

THE GRAND ALLIANCE OF RICH AND POOR

Once our hypothetical patient has used his capital to buy himself a more meaningful life, the idea does not need to end. The similarities between the very rich and the very poor have already been discussed. Perhaps our newly successful executive will experience an awakened sense of purpose in life. When people make discoveries the urge is strong to share them.

THE GRAND ALLIANCE OF RICH AND POOR

If the very wealthy young man wishes to share his discovery of what the imaginative use of capital can do, the logical recipients of his discovery would be others from his own class with similar problems, and the very poor. Middle-class individuals could certainly be benefited by imaginative investments of capital in people, but they don't actually need it as badly. The preservation of the middle-class identification insures a certain direction and energy for their life.

Why should the very rich be interested in helping the poor? Are they not so used to seeing them as servants that they are completely out of touch with their problems? Perhaps that is an advantage. After all, prejudice and discrimination are the results of fear, and the rich have less fear of the very poor than does the middle class. The poor have been known as willing servants; they have not been seen as potential competitors for jobs as they are by the middle class. If a generalization were to be made, it would seem that the rich have tended to be indifferent to the poor, though of course there are those with greater and lesser degrees of social awareness. Lacking a fear of this segment of society might make the rich the ideal catalysts for social change.

The very rich, like the middle class, are afraid of revolution. But it has been the middle class that has most threatened the position of the rich. They are out to reach their august pinnacle, and that involves reducing the exclusive status of the rich. The snobbishness of the rich toward the new arrivals to positions of great wealth is an indication of the threat they feel. While there may be some fear of the poor, the greatest anxiety has traditionally been toward "foreigners" and middle-class radicals.

How receptive would the hard-core black poor, for exsimple, be to receiving help from the very rich? I suspect that would be the least of the problems. The militants who would bring down the system would of course not be receptive; but they have already formed some identification with the middle class—albeit a negative one—and have a plan for obtaining certain goals. In terms of power—and often education, too—the militant leaders are not the ones who need the help.

The poor who have worked as servants know the rich as kindly or indifferent employers. More likely they know the rich not at all. The bigoted hardhat is an infinitely more familiar figure to them. The long years of oppression have left their scars on the poor in terms of deep fears and great hostility. But I propose that the rich might be able more effectively to approach them than the middle class has been. The rich do not have as much guilt concerning the poor as does the middle class; this is because of their long indifference and the different kind of conscience they possess. And the absence of guilt should make for improved communications.

The lower classes have learned to recognize the guilt which the middle class feels toward them. Although the guilt is often mixed with a sincere desire to be helpful, its presence often interferes with the effecting of help. When a person attempts to help another person toward whom he feels considerable guilt, the possibilities open to him become more limited. For example, guilt might motivate our help-provider to demand less of the recipient than he is capable of.

The recipients, on their part, have often learned to exploit the guilt which is felt toward them. It is, after all, human nature to take the easiest course. And if the guilty help-givers can be maneuvered to give much and demand little, it is natural to prefer that. But the result often is that less is expected of the poor than they are capable of, and the poor and their would-be helpers unwittingly conspire together to perpetuate a damaging paternalistic attitude.

There is no implication intended that the problems of the poor can be solved if they were treated in a less paternalistic manner. That is obviously not true. But it must be recognized that among the poor there are those who are capable of far more than is expected of them. Instrumentalities for helping them often become encrusted in bureaucratic rigidity and are rendered ineffective. The loss is suffered by all the poor, but perhaps the greatest loss is suffered by the more gifted among them.

I know of one very wealthy woman who finally resolved her boredom by becoming deeply committed to an art center in a ghetto. She had a deep appreciation for art and was able to recognize those among the underprivileged who had creative talent. She became the patroness for several artists and coaxed and demanded their best efforts from them. One or two have become successful. Could this approach not also be extended to the business world?

In this fantasy it is hypothesized that the rich could seek out those with promise from among the poor. They could hire experts to search out potential leaders or those possessed with particular attributes. Furthermore it is hypothesized that our rich helper could effectively approach the gifted poor with his proposal. The plans would of course have infinite possible variations, but they would have a common basic intent. The poor recipient would be offered a chance to work closely with the rich donor to prepare him for a high-level position in business.

Whatever education might be required for this position would be supplied by experts hired for this purpose. Whatever social training was required would be supplied by the rich donor and his staff. The absence of guilt would make for no-nonsense, realistic expectations, and I suspect there would be a good chance of these expectations being met. The two crucial factors would seem to be the careful selection of trainees with high potential and the guilt-free demand that they use this potential fully.

The concluding portion of this fantasy involves a more broadly based expansion of this plan. Those who successfully complete it would be catapulted into positions of leadership for other poor. The barriers to progress would then be challenged from above as they are now from below. Those of lesser potential would be invited into programs that would train them for positions they are capable of. As the fantasy grows more grandiose and then trails off, a huge self-help apparatus is envisioned. But short of this expansiveness, a one-to-one helping relationship between rich and poor does not seem too farfetched a fantasy.

21
CORs ANONYMOUS

THE FINAL IDEA HAS TO DO WITH THE CREATION OF AN alliance of CORs who are in—or have been in—the same boat. While not as appealing in a social sense as the idea of reaching down and yanking up members of the poor, it is probably more easily accomplished and is also concerned with the salvage of wasted resources.

In the discussion of the golden ghetto it was pointed out

how socially clannish the COR families tend to be. But there is considerable contact between them in terms of financial and political connections. Those whose wealth arose from the moving picture industry, for example, have a wide familiarity with most of the other "top" families in that industry. The same is true for steel, banking, and so on. The very wealthy often have surprising access to others of wealth, in a manner analogous to the immediate access and fraternal feelings shared by the medical profession.

This fraternity of the rich would make the formation of a group such as CORs Anonymous possible. The founding leaders would be CORs who have recognized their dysgradia and learned to overcome it—either through psychiatric treatment or through self-help and fortunate life experiences. One way or another they have found a way to make their lives more meaningful and wish to help others. Word is sent through the fraternity of the existence of the organization and secret sufferers are invited to join. The more blatant sufferers are directly recruited.

What about the reactions of the COR parents? For several reasons I do not think it would be particularly negative. First of all, the families are one generation closer to their middle-class identifications; quite often they are less afflicted with dysgradia, and they might well appreciate an offer to help them with their children. There is further appeal in having that offer of help come from within their own fraternity. But even without the approval of their parents the CORs would probably be receptive; after all they are not as tied to their parents' values as is middle-class youth.

And what would CORs Anonymous offer? The considerable success of Alcoholics Anonymous rests in part on the recognition that for a large group of alcoholics there is no hope for cure. Thus a permanent apparatus exists to constantly reinforce a new life-style. In an analogous sense, the problem of dysgradia is more often lived with than cured. A more or less permanent defect exists, and the remedying of that defect cannot be deliberately accomplished. The successfully treated COR has learned to live with and overcome a more or less permanent handicap, though passing years and gratifying life experiences may alter that situation.

One life event that can alter a state of dysgradia is marriage. While the CORs tend to marry within the clan and fear those who are too different, an occasional exception occurs. Love sometimes pairs a COR with a middle-class partner. There is the possibility that the middle-class partner will be swallowed up by the easy life and forsake his background. But if he is not entering the marriage simply to elevate his social status, a "therapeutic" situation may develop.

Suppose a COR takes an upper-middle-class wife, and a deep feeling of love exists between them. Since childhood the wife has valued hard work, gainful activities, creativity, and so forth. She may then unconsciously—though sometimes quite deliberately—have expectations for her spouse that are new to him. To the extent that his inertia is due to an absence of meaningful identifications rather than neurotic blocks, he may be able to fulfill these expectations. The appreciation of a spouse, as a constructive motivating force, must not be underestimated.

A similar situation is possible with a group such as CORs Anonymous. Whereas the middle-class therapist must be very careful not to attempt to impart his middle-class standards to his patients, CORs do not have the same restrictions.

They all have a similar background and hence would not be attempting to enforce ideals that make no sense in terms of their actual life situation. This immediately makes new ideas more acceptable.

Like a marriage, a group of COR-peers could commit themselves to a permanent "contract." Those who have been helped would take the initiative in helping the new members to understand the nature of their problem. The psychological and material resources of the group would be utilized in working out plans for developing the potential of the member being helped. This neophyte would be paired with a member who has already achieved a new life pattern who would then help implement the plan.

The pairing would be done after the potentials, interests, and talents of the neophyte were carefully evaluated. The helper would be responsible for leading the recipient at a reasonable pace in carrying out the plan. The pressure of the entire peer group, which can be tremendous, would be brought to bear upon any backsliders. The group would literally force the neophyte into a more meaningful life direction and keep him there. The approval of a peer group is an immensely gratifying force.

There is a distinction between this kind of peer-group help and that offered by more conventional analytical group psychotherapy. The several CORs I have known who have had group therapy have encountered problems that limited the help they received. There is the problem of the very real differences in background between the CORs and the usual participant in a group. The latter are largely from middle-class backgrounds. There is no possibility of a true peer relationship.

The middle-class members of the group tend to react with an unavoidable degree of hostile envy. They tend to be outraged at the CORs' lack of occupation and goals. Not appreciating the fact that such values are not really needed, they attack him for laziness and self-indulgence. His lessened conflicts about assertiveness and sexuality make it difficult for the COR to empathize with the more typical problems the other members of the group are working on. This in turn increases the distance between them.

Granting that a group of typical middle-class patients is not very helpful to the COR, why not a group composed entirely of CORs? In a sense that should be more successful, and that is the basic idea of CORs Anonymous. But a conventional group of CORs would be very difficult to arrange. They tend to live farther away from the usual centers where therapists practice, and they are after all relatively few in number. A dedicated self-help group could have flexibility enough to make the endeavor practical. They could arrange to fly across country en masse when a member needed help and could enlist professional help when needed.

If such an organization could come into existence, it would have the potential for salvaging many CORs who are otherwise destined to lead pointless lives and contribute nothing to the world. Utilizing the help of a group possessing such immense resources, a source of wasted energy could be tapped.

22

THE SUCCESSFUL RICH

> *I believe that every right implies a responsibility; every opportunity, an obligation; every possession, a duty.*
> JOHN D. ROCKEFELLER, JR.

NOT ALL CHILDREN OF THE RICH ARE CORS. THAT DESIGnation was reserved for those who suffer from dysgradia. This group of individuals, with such great potential and with so little purpose in life, deserves our special attention. But what about that large group of the rich whose lives would be considered successful? What can we learn from them which might help the CORs?

At first glance, one might conclude that the successful rich have retained enough middle-class values to supply a healthy direction for living. And indeed this is usually true for the first generations after the great wealth was acquired. These first generations are close enough to their middle-class origins that their problems are likely to be more typically neurotic. The first generation was closely identified with the founder of the family fortune and is concerned with continuing his work and securing the new position. His children are more likely to pass through a crucial period of identity crisis.

These identity problems typically occur during the second —sometimes the third—generation in the history of the newly wealthy family. The middle-class values no longer are meaningful and something must be found to replace them. Hard work to earn a living is no longer necessary. Thrift, industry, careful planning for the future—these values are part of the family tradition, but no longer make sense in terms of their way of life.

Tension at this point often arises between the younger and older generations. The son sees the father working extremely hard in the family business and cannot understand why; the business will run without him, and there is no need for acquiring more money. The father sees his son becoming more pleasure-oriented and renouncing the values he had held dear. Sensing the dangerous emptiness beginning to develop in his son, he clings all the more firmly to the old values. The outcome can go in several different directions.

If the father has enough control over the son's life, he may enforce a certain life-style as long as he lives. But that offers no real solution. If he cannot exercise that kind of control, the son may rebel and lead a disruptive kind of life. If there is enough guilt he may become depressed or destructively impulsive. What may appear from the outside to be a wanton, pleasure-oriented life may actually be a desperate effort to escape the anxiety of the threatening personality disruption. There is no longer a point to the old ideals; there is nothing to replace them; without internal sources for supplying gratification it is sought in the outside world. The pleasures derived cannot be enjoyed because of guilt, and a complete breakdown may occur. The children of this transitional generation cannot avoid dysgradia. It is at this point in the family history that it begins.

If this transitional generation can pass through the crucial identity crisis and establish a satisfactory modification in identifications, a much more fortunate outcome is possible. This generation must accomplish a great deal. Many of the old middle-class values must be finally renounced. Their wealth is a fact that cannot be denied; work can no longer be motivated by financial need. A change in the conscience and ideals must be accomplished—there is no reason to feel guilty for spending money and enjoying luxury. If these values can be renounced and the conscience altered, something must fill the void. This is accomplished by the successful rich.

The essential factor in the successful transition from middle class to upper class involves the establishment of a new system for maintaining self-esteem. If the old values no longer are a basis for deriving internal gratification, a new basis must be found. There are some old values that can be successfully altered. The importance of the parental role is classless, and the successful rich have notably close-knit families. If going to work is no longer meaningful, spending time with one's children and helping them develop their potential remains gratifying.

The heightened importance of family life can be expanded to a helpful attitude toward the larger community of man. This may be the origin of the philanthropic and public service activities that characterize the lives of the successful rich. To help one's fellowman is a value that pervades the middle class; it is eclipsed for most by the values more closely connected with earning a living. This value can become the basis for tremendous gratification for the wealthy.

If one studies the lives of the successful rich, one notes a tendency toward activities in three areas: philanthropy, public service, and creative business. The first two would seem to be outgrowths of an enhancement of the Judaeo-Christian ideal of helping one's fellowman, with or without a religious basis. The philanthropic and public service activities of the Rockefellers and Kennedys are obvious examples. Less dramatic but similarly valuable and gratifying lives are led by many of the less well known rich.

The successful rich who remain active in business activities have developed a new value concerning them. They have drawn upon the outcome of the rivalry between son and father, brother and brother, to derive motivation and gratification from the challenge of competition. While this is also an element in the middle-class work orientation, it becomes the primary motive for these successful rich. Business activities are now a game, a competitive challenge. There is gratification in outdoing a competitor, in exceeding last year's profits. The motive is very similar to that seen in competitive sports. The element of the contest or game is also a major part of the political activities referred to previously.

Less often, one encounters very wealthy people who have developed certain creative talents into highly productive and meaningful lives. For them creativity in such areas as art and science becomes the basis of an extremely gratifying existence. On occasion, the discovery and development of such a talent has been the key to escape from the golden ghetto.

Once the transitional generations have established a firm identity as unashamed rich and have developed new value systems for deriving personal gratification, these can become part of the family heritage and passed from generation to generation. These fortunate families now have a meaningful set of roles to pass on to succeeding generations.

With the strengthening of family life, there is enough contact for the young to identify with their parents' values. Thus a logical series of life steps can be transmitted which may be quite different from those of the successful middle class, but may be equally effective in providing the framework for a meaningful life.

If business activities still are important in the family, the children will automatically assume that they will arrive at positions of power and responsibility while they are fairly young. They will begin developing role preimages which are in harmony with the actual realities of their future. This will be reflected in play—a major indicator of the kind of self-images the child is developing. He may play games in which he is an executive, an important government official, or some other personage of high achievement. He will begin to demonstrate an ability to use his authority without the common middle-class conflicts about aggressiveness. Ideals concerning the responsible management of capital will replace ideals involved with advancement through a business organization.

Where business activities have diminished as important parts of identity formation, a variety of other activities can fill the need. Raising horses, boat racing, political activities, and philanthropic pursuits are a few of the directions the family interests may follow. Some of these will conflict with the typical middle-class ideals of the kinds of activities that are valued, but they may be completely in harmony with the actual realities of the upper-class milieu.

The transitional generation can go either way. A successful resolution of the identity crisis may establish a family renowned for its philanthropy, business activities, or public service. A failure of resolution sets up the makings of a family suffering from dysgradia. When family closeness is not highly valued, the uninterested pattern of rearing children tremendously enhances the defect.

23

PREVENTION

Certain thoughts concerning the prevention of dysgradia may be derived from the study of families who have avoided it and from CORs who have been treated. There are also implications for the prevention of certain problems more usual to the middle class.

The key figure in prevention would be the founder of the family fortune. Unfortunately that approach is not going to help the present COR sufferers. But America is still the land of opportunity and new fortunes are constantly being made. A heightened awareness on the part of these men of the possible problems that lie in store for their families may cause them to give greater attention to the changes that are occurring. As old values become less important, new values must be developed. Above all, the importance of the family unit must be recognized and preserved.

The early generations can be alert to the problems of the transitional generations. That changes in values are occurring must be accepted, even though the elders do not feel comfortable with the changes.

"My family is rich now. I was happy to get a bicycle, and now my son has a bright red sports car. He won't need to work the way I did, but how can I help keep him from becoming a playboy?" Just asking this question makes that occurrence a lot less likely. An acceptance of change enables a closeness to remain between the generations, and a total repudiation of all the old ideals is avoided. There is then a chance for modifications and shifting emphasis in the old ideals to occur. The transitional generation then need not become demoralized through a lack of meaningful identifications.

Unfortunately, the founders of great fortunes usually do not recognize their moment in the history of their family. They are too occupied with what is happening, too excited with the changes in their lives, to think about the implications of these changes. It is more likely that helpful prevention may be effected at later stages in the progression.

Where the transitional generation has not successfully weathered its crises, the children will have some degree of identity impairment. Hence the young of the transitional generation should be recognized as pivotal in the future course of the family. When the elders recognize what is happening, they can do a great deal to alleviate the problem. When this group comes for psychiatric treatment, there is an important opportunity, not only for helping one individual, but also for preventing problems for future generations.

The problems presented by this transitional generation are not yet dysgradia. They have identified with enough of the old values to be torn by conflict. The clinical pictures they present may involve impulsive acting-out, depression, and various degrees of self-destructive life-styles. Their problems are more familiar to psychotherapists and resemble the syndromes of neuroses of mobility. The treatment is usually more conventional psychoanalytic therapy, with special attention to the identity confusion and conflict over values. Sometimes both generations need to be involved in the therapy.

I saw Ted, a twenty-seven-year-old man of Armenian extraction, a few years ago for a consultation. His father had become wealthy through an aggressively run importing business. The two men were involved in constant fights—sometimes verging on violence. The problems began when Ted started working in the business. The father felt Ted was lazy and incompetent; Ted felt his father was rigid, unimaginative, and unable to delegate responsibility.

Ted had begun to drink heavily and suffered episodes of severe depression. He frequently was unable to go to work, leading to a new round of conflict with his father. It became apparent that he did not have the drive his father had or the same degree of concern with detail. He was sincerely interested in the business, but saw himself as a modern executive. He could not understand why his father would go down to the warehouse to help unload a new shipment of merchandise.

Why the two men differed so much in their approach was clear: Father had worked his way up from a penniless immigrant, while Ted had a college degree in business. The father's values were straightforward ones he derived from an old country family of merchants. Ted had had enough exposure to his father to develop some identification with his values, but he grew up in a wealthy neighborhood exposed to those more concerned with enjoying wealth than acquiring it. He felt ashamed of his father, and that produced tremendous guilt. More guilt was added by his inability to share his father's total involvement with the business. The result was the self-destructive drinking and depression.

Ted had recently married and was the father of twin sons. As I listened to the description of the problem, my thoughts kept turning to this third generation. They would be in serious difficulty, surely suffering dysgradia in addition to whatever other problems they might develop, if their father continued his self-destructive course.

I asked to see Ted's father. He was angry and anxious about coming in; he felt psychiatrists were for crazy people, and neither he nor his son was crazy. As I explained my view of the problem he and his son were having, he relaxed and began an animated dialogue about his rags-to-riches career and his son's laziness. He accepted my recommendation that the three of us meet together.

We met weekly for about a year. The problem could not be completely resolved—there was simply too much distance between the two men's psychological makeup. But the gap was narrowed, and they each made some accommodation to the other. The beginning disruption of Ted's life was stopped, and the drinking and depression were no longer problems. The future of the family seemed more hopeful.

Members of wealthy groups, and all groups for that matter, who are concerned about the future of their children can do much to avoid the demoralizing effects of the malady we have been concerned with. A great deal changes almost automatically when parents become aware of the effects of their life-style on their children. I am not referring to the overanxious, overprotective concern that cripples, but to a simple degree of heightened awareness that is too often absent.

When parents wander around depressed, drinking heavily, and bored to desperation, the effects on their children are obviously harmful. An awakening concern for their children helps them begin to help themselves. Children can be a bother, and with great wealth one can hire the "best," but the "best" is often woefully bad. That awareness must be disseminated among the wealthy. They need to rediscover their children. A small shift in life-style—more meals together, listening more carefully to what ideas their children are developing about their purpose in life, simply more time with them—can begin an important shift in direction. Aside from helping the children, this shift can reawaken a sense of purpose in life for the parents.

Children derive ideas about the world from exposure to other children. The children of the wealthy are often extremely isolated, either because of geography, their parents' fear of those outside their little circle, or indifference on the part of the parents. A need to share experiences with a peer group is overlooked—and by peer group is meant other children of similar age and development, not necessarily social class.

Wealthy parents tend to send their children to private schools that are often simply an extension of the golden ghetto. Whether in the long run they receive a better education or not is a moot point. But there are ample opportunities for them to have exposure to a wider cross section of the world they will be living in. Scouting, YMCA, organized sports, museum clubs, orchestras—the potential list is endless and is limited only by the child's interests and endowments and the parents' imagination. Exposure to activities outside the golden ghetto will have a healthy effect on the child. He will learn that being rich does not carry enough value in itself. Competition, cooperation, and working toward long-range goals can be awakened by exposing the child to a broader cross section of the world than can be provided in his family's private little world.

Finally, parents must become aware of the tremendous amount of time their children are spending with hired help and the great potential for damage that exists in that situation. Even where a greater awareness of the importance of the family to the child is awakened, it is not likely that the rich will do away with servants entirely. Hence the need to cultivate a greater awareness of the kind of people who are hired, and of what goes on between them and the children when all is quiet. A smooth, quietly running household is not proof in itself that all is well.

In sum, the greatest force for preventing demoralized youth is a reawakening of the importance of the parental role. Too many among the very wealthy have forgotten that simple truth.

24

NEUROSES OF MOBILITY

THERE IS A SPECIAL SET OF PROBLEMS THAT IS SEEN with increasing frequency in the children of new arrivals at the top of the middle class. These might be called *mobility neuroses*. They are related to the conflicts between the solid middle-class values the children were inculcated with and the different values encountered as the family reaches upper-middle-class levels. Here we shift the focus a bit, from the full-blown state of dysgradia with its deficiency in role images, to a condition in which conflicting role images produce turmoil.

The middle-class values are ancient and have proved highly adaptive for our society. As one moves upward there is a definite change. Industriousness, hard work, and thrift become less important, while status, glamour, and material possessions become more important. No single factor can account for this turn toward materialism and superficiality. This shift is related partly to the fact that man desires to find value in his work in order to maintain his self-esteem. For some who have made rapid upward moves in their status, their means of earning a living seem trivial and without value as they become more removed from the direct supplying of goods and services.

This decrease in one's work-pride accounts in part for the increased emphasis on status. However, those whose work does seem to provide them with considerable gratification do not seem immune. Other factors must be involved. A major one has to do with envy. The members of the upper middle class are able to earn enough money to live as well as the upper class—almost. They can afford payments on grand homes; they can afford servants and travel. They are almost rich. They are *almost* accepted by the rich. But they aren't.

The truly rich are beyond their reach. While some of the arrivistes may eventually make it, most will never be so secure that they need never work. Perhaps this envy of a position that seems within reach and yet so unattainable creates this need for status. Bigger houses, larger boats, more expensive automobiles, grander parties, more beautiful new wives—perhaps these will demonstrate that one has *arrived*.

The most important reason for this nouveau riche caricature lies, I believe, in a defense against self-hate and shame. One's earliest identifications tend to last a lifetime. A child born into a humble middle-class family sees himself in that status. Take for an example the son of a hardworking carpenter. Now, through the wonders of state universities, parental sacrifice, and talent he is a very prosperous Beverly Hills attorney. He lives in an elegant house, has servants, all of that, and yet in his heart he is the carpenter's son.

This secret feeling of being a fraud, of not really belonging where he appears to be, is a constant threat to the new arrivals. Hence the effort to cover up this self-shame by a gaudy denial of shame. Big tip to the manicurist, pinch the ass of the receptionist, demand a better table at Chasen's—all this a vain effort to deny a secret shame. "What am I doing here? My father lives on a union pension and speaks working-class English. And that's what I spoke until law school. Who am I kidding?"

It is difficult to describe this shame, but it is pervasive. The exploitation of it by clever entrepreneurs supports many businesses. These enterprising restaurateurs, barbers, hairdressers, and boutique operators have discovered that what comes easily is not valued. Therefore, they are haughty and aloof, if not downright rude, to the obviously prosperous newcomers. And the newcomers eat it up; they must spend enough and return often enough to be *recognized*.

This search for status, whether born out of a loss of work gratification, envy, or secret shame, pervades the lives of many who have achieved rapid upward mobility. The children are the ones most likely to suffer from it. The parents are too busy playing the game to note what is happening to them. But the children are caught in a difficult identity crisis.

The parents are sustained by their basic middle-class values. They know they have accomplished something, they are successes. The status seeking adds a little to their self-esteem—the thrill of being recognized at Perino's—but in large measure serves to ward off shame and inferiority feelings. But the status seeking occupies so great a portion of their lives that the children can't help but identify with it. And status-hungry parents are not above using their children to advance their aims—encouraging them to associate with the elite of their group and to try for the most prestigious schools.

The children cannot fall back on any sense of success or achievement. They have heard the stories of Father's success, but it wasn't theirs. They have an identification with the role of working hard and becoming successful like Father, and hence have something that the CORs lack. But that industrious identification conflicts with the indolent status seeking they see all around them. "Work hard, go to college, become something, prepare to take over Father's business" is hard to reconcile with "Get invited to the movie star's daughter's party, wow them with your new sports car, have your hair styled by Dad's barber."

The status-seeking way of life is very seductive, though often exhausting. When one "in" place is no longer "in," find the new one. It's expensive but the parents are generous. Why worry, study, cram, compete, save, plan, anticipate, and wait? It's here now! Sex, money, glamour—status. For some, this conflict is disastrous. The parents, preoccupied with their status seeking, are swept up by the apparent glamour of their children's lives. Through the children they can escape their secret shame, the children have no humble past to live down.

The parents tend to assume that the middle-class values that got them where they are will likewise take care of their children. But they overlook the seductiveness of the "good life." Too late they begin to be concerned about poor school performance, petty delinquency, the absence of future plans. They suddenly become aware that something is radically wrong, and sometimes they panic. The values that sustained them seem in jeopardy. As with the renewed religious fervor that attends efforts at suppression, they are suddenly firebrands for homely values.

The parental panic hits against a dormant conflict of identifications. The young adult spent his childhood with George Washington and Abraham Lincoln, but his adolescence with Frank Sinatra. There is already some shame about the surrender to the "good life," but it is suppressed by the frantic effort to "keep up." When the parents come charging in, talking about college and working in Father's office, there is bound to be an explosion. The parents, warding off their own guilt, react with righteous indignation and speak of laziness and ingratitude. The "generation gap" becomes a chasm.

The child in this situation has several possible directions open to him. He might acquiesce, buckle down, and satisfy his parents', and his own secret, wishes. If not, a crisis results that can be resolved in a variety of ways or can become chronic.

The young adult is angry. He feels betrayed by his parents who taught him what they now condemn. His guilt about his own pleasure seeking is projected onto them, and they

NEUROSES OF MOBILITY

stand accused of hypocrisy. He may resolve this conflict by a major shift in his life-style. He may become manifestly neurotic or attempt to fight out his inner turmoil by going to war against his family. Though there may be any of the innumerable symptoms that one encounters in a severe identity crisis, there is usually considerable evidence of internal conflict—hence the designation "mobility neurosis."

An almost universal feature of this neurosis of mobility is depression. It may be simply that, a depressive neurosis; the great loss of self-esteem produces the regression that results in depression. More often, the acute depression is warded off by some form of acting-out or character distortion. One sees a tragically large number of such youths living a frantic life of compromise: desperately seeking pleasure and constantly hurting themselves by not accepting any real satisfaction. This masochistic pattern is sometimes difficult to recognize from the outside. Only in the analyst's consulting room does the suffering become apparent. Without treatment, their children will very likely develop dysgradia. This life of turmoil cannot supply children the necessary images for identification.

Sometimes the guilt is unbearable and the youth feels he must break completely with his family. But what masquerades as a meaningful new life-style may be only a group of frightened, lonely young people trying to reassure one another that their alienation is an important new movement. That they are living out a neurotic conflict is betrayed by their noisy protestations, their extremism, and their determination to hurt their parents, and by the many evidences of self-destructiveness. This effort at solution lasts only as long as a group holds together.

The child of the rich suffering from dysgradia has no such

internal conflict. He may have some areas of neurotic conflict, but he does not have the major identity conflict that characterizes the mobility neuroses. The latter are much more amenable to conventional psychoanalytic treatment, and the prognosis is much more hopeful than for the CORs. For underneath the anger, alienation, and confusion are certain middle-class values that can form a foundation for future growth.

The problems of this group are quite similar in many ways to those of the transitional generation of the newly rich. Both groups are torn between different sets of values, but there is a major difference. The transitional generation no longer needs many of the old middle-class values and must find new values and modify old ones drastically. Only by such a major change can a stable system for maintaining self-esteem be arrived at. This is not the case with the middle-class youth caught in a mobility conflict. His basic middle-class values can still be highly adaptive for his life circumstances. A conflict is much easier to resolve than a void.

The story of John is fairly typical of mobility neurosis.

25

JOHN

John's grandfather Jacob was born in an East European ghetto. He came to the United States with his wife and one infant son. They lived with relatives in a New York ghetto, where Jacob scraped out a meager living as a tailor. In their New World ghetto five more sons were born, the last one claiming the life of Grandmother. An aunt, weary with the burdens of her own family, did her duty to raise this family. And what a family!

Jacob was not bitter long at losing his wife. He was too busy sewing. His role in life was clear, and had been unchanged for centuries—to work hard, study the Torah and Talmud, and provide his sons a trade for earning a living and as much education as possible. A formula that was unchanged for centuries. And in America the education could reach beyond Torah and Talmud to the university. Bitter? In a millennium nobody in his family had had the opportunity to so live up to his ordained role.

The oldest, Adam, worked with his father, learned tailoring, with his father opened a small factory making dresses, and helped put the next five through college—three doctors and two lawyers. When Jacob died Adam moved to Los Angeles, opened a dress factory, and married a simple woman with a background similar to his. Their only child was John. The business prospered, making Adam very wealthy and moving the family to Beverly Hills.

Adam's home was beautiful. On one side lived Mr. Sanders, a film distributor, and on the other was a park. John liked Mr. Sanders, a big, friendly extrovert. But he didn't care much for his wife, a bleached blond who had been an actress. He avoided looking at her for fear she would see his eyes observing her low-cut necklines. She laughed a lot, but there was a shrillness that grated on his ears. John was a bright and happy little boy, not handsome, but neither were his parents. In spite of the acquired wealth, his first eight years were quite like the early years of his forebears. The family attended Friday night services, he was overfed and given violin lessons, and great emphasis was placed on his studies.

As Father's wealth increased, a gradual change began. The Friday night services were forgotten, and only the High

JOHN

Holidays were observed. Adam began to change; his bald head now sported a toupee, his gray moustache was dyed black, and he spent many weekends in Las Vegas entertaining customers. John began to hear arguments at night. One night he heard his mother say, "Adam, you don't come to me. Why?"

"Sarah, you know I'm working hard and I'm tired."

Her quiet, sad voice continued, "I can survive that, but you aren't giving enough to John. He needs more of you."

"I'm tired of that, Sarah! My father spent his life sewing and his children did OK, didn't they? He wasn't no Boy Scout leader, so we're bums? He and I are pals, so don't worry."

John was eleven then. Alone in his bed, lying in the dark, he knew there was trouble coming. He loved his father and had been close to him until this change started. Now he felt frightened and sad. "Why does Daddy seem different to Momma? He always rushes out—I seem a nuisance to him." His young mind perceived a great deal.

When John was twelve the bomb exploded. Mother was in New York visiting her family, and John had enjoyed the week together with his father. It was summer vacation and Father had been in a festive mood—going to work later and taking John out to breakfast. Father was coming home early, and they'd seen three movies together. It was the last evening before Mother returned, and the maid had served dinner by the pool. John was thinking Father seemed more like he used to. Then suddenly—

"Son, you're not a baby anymore—so I can be frank. Your mother and I are getting a divorce—we just don't love each other anymore." John felt dizzy and nauseated.

"You'll stay here with Mother like you always have—

nothing will change." Tears were welling up now. "We'll spend time together—you and me—just like always."

John could only murmur, "Sure, sure. Why?"

"Why, Son? You're gonna hear a lot of gossip, so get it straight from me. Daisy Sanders and I have fallen in love . . ."

The dizziness was now being replaced by a sensation of heat. He felt hot all over and was trembling.

John thought, That must be why they moved! That blond, with the tits? Daddy? Oh my God!

"Son, we live in an age when people aren't prudes anymore, you'll understand when you're older."

I'll never understand, John thought.

The conversation lasted awhile longer but John's memory of it was spotty. Grief, fear, and hurt—with only very brief flashes of anger—left him in a daze. He remembered Father calling Daisy and saying, "Sure, I told him and he's fine—a real sport—I'll put him on. Son, it would be nice if you said something to Daisy—she's worried you'll hate her—imagine!" John remembers the phone thrust at him, mumbling something noncommittal, and getting outside as soon as he could while Father talked on to Daisy.

Divorce wasn't that rare among his peers, and he'd known there was trouble between his father and mother, but he hadn't realized it had reached that state. "And with Daisy! That means Dad has gone to bed with her!" He tried to remember how it used to be. Dad's bald head and smiling face with his arm around Mother. "When was that? My birthday—lots of times—that's how it always was before."

John thought about Mother. "They must have planned it

so he could spend the week with me and tell me about Daisy. What a rotten, stupid idea! Build me up with a great week for this! The goddamned fool! The son of a bitch! Oh, my poor mother." The thought of his mother being left alone, that simple, kind woman left for that flashy blond, tore at his insides. John didn't realize it then, but that evening marked the culmination of a process that had begun a few years before. That was the final hurt that caused the building up of a defensive system that changed his life.

Obviously all boys whose parents divorce do not suffer such damaging personality changes. In John's case, a series of unfortunate circumstances had set up a dangerous predisposition. His father was an aggressive, hard-driving businessman; his mother a warm kind gentle woman. John as a little boy found it difficult to handle the normal angry feelings that children feel toward their fathers. He went through a period of great anxiety at around four or five related to envy and anger at his father's powerful position and frightening fears of retaliation. In his nightmares he was chased by angry policemen, clearly symbols of Father as the enforcer of the repression of his hostile feelings.

John resolved this rather typical childhood conflict by renouncing, for the time being at least, his early aggressive masculine strivings; he moved toward a more passive identification with his mother. While this was clearly a defensive reaction to his fear of his aggressive urges, it left him turning more toward aesthetic pursuits and away from more masculine kinds of competition. He became very concerned with his violin lessons and very interested in the theatre. He adopted a more passive, submissive attitude toward his father; by repressing the normal rivalry with Father he was left with a strong awareness of his love feelings.

The changes in Father in the few years preceding the divorce were particularly disruptive for John. The passive, compliant little boy who loved his father would probably have come out without serious damage if things had proceeded normally. A loving relationship with a father deeply involved in his son's future would have helped guide him into activities that would prepare him for business or a career. A good relationship with a peer group would have helped reinforce masculine endeavors and put limits on the degree of aesthetic interests. Unfortunately, this was not the case.

Adam was unusually vulnerable to the new status-seeking way of life. Probably he harbored some bitterness for having to work so young to send his brothers to school, and perhaps this resentment made him less sensitive to his son's needs. Having a beautiful former actress actively interested in him was more than he could resist; a long tradition of stable family life—with emphasis on child rearing—seemed less gratifying on that street in Beverly Hills than the glamour of a love nest with Daisy. And probably he was deeply ashamed of his humble origins.

So there was John, during his first seven or eight years taught to value family ties and education, to turn toward Father in a somewhat passive manner for guidance, but beginning to notice a change in Father's values. Suddenly Father seemed more interested in his appearance, in his tailored clothes, in celebrities in their home, than in his wife and son. A bitterness began to develop in John, a confusion of who he was and where he was going. His early learning and strong identification with his mother's values made it impossible for him to accept or identify with his father's new directions. A beginning tendency toward fighting his father in very subtle passive ways was quite apparent by the time he was ten years old. He would go down to Father's factory to work during a summer vacation and infuriate him by his slowness and his frequent mistakes. Father would get angry but he was already too disconnected from the family to confront this problem effectively.

Between ten and twelve John's grades declined from As to Bs, his interests were more strongly in the arts, his friends were a more passive group of boys. These changes bothered his father, and he let John know it. John secretly was pleased that he had one weapon for eliciting a concerned look from him. After the divorce these trends increased until John had perfected a method of fighting his father, and all his father figures, in a passive manner. In reconstructing the years after the divorce, John pondered Mother's apparent acceptance of his tremendously self-destructive passive-aggressiveness. Perhaps Mother's hurt at Father for forsaking her blinded her to her son's behavior and caused her unconsciously to share in the subtle reproach to him of John's downhill drift.

And downhill John drifted. He was never openly committed to a homosexual orientation himself, but by the time he was fifteen many of the friends he had chosen were, and this upset Adam deeply. John played a game of defending them to his father on their every-other-weekend outings. Driving to the country club in Father's Cadillac on a Saturday morning just before his sixteenth birthday, John heard Father demand, "Who was that boy—I think it was a boy—you were talking to when I drove up?"

"That was Thad."

"Thad?"

"Yes—short for Thaddeus."

"Oh." And then after a few minutes Father continued, "He seemed sort of funny to me."

John smiled, "Oh, he's an artist, you know how they are."

"I'm not sure I know how they are. How is this Thad?"

"You mean is he queer? Yes—at school he's known as a screaming faggot."

"I appreciate your openness, Son. So why are you and he so chummy?"

"I like him."

The pattern had developed so insidiously and become so nearly automatic that John often was not aware of what he was doing. This time he knew he was deliberately provoking his father, and his heart was pounding. He had to play this carefully so that his father's maximum apprehension and anger would be reached just as they arrived at the club where the subject would be dropped and Father would be smiling and slapping backs.

After another pause, "You like him? Don't his mannerisms and his reputation bother you?"

"No." John was hiding his anxiety with a grin.

John was deeply involved in his analysis before he fully understood the passive, self-destructive methods he used to attack Father, and why he had used them. But although largely unaware of what he was doing, he had become an expert in provoking him to the burning point by the time he was fifteen.

"Goddamn it, John, you're not a fag and you shouldn't hang out with them." Father was close to fury, and John was feeling triumphant.

JOHN

"But, Dad," he said softly and calmly, "he's the most gifted set designer I know."

"I'm not talking about his talent—granted he can turn out a nice set of something—but it isn't good for you to only associate with such effeminate . . ."

And so it would go, Father angry at John's passive responses—he'd have been so happy if John had gotten excited and yelled—and secretly worried that his only child would become homosexual. John wouldn't give his father any reassurance that he was not drifting into homosexuality, and relished his anguish.

The hostility to Father at times became more open, and then it frightened John. He was having dinner with Daisy and Father to celebrate his seventeenth birthday when Father brought the subject up again.

"Son, Daisy and I have been discussing why you don't go out more with girls."

"Yes, Dad?"

"I hope you won't take this wrong, but do you know you'd be much more attractive if you just had a little work done on your nose? And your ears should be pulled back a little. Daisy was telling me, some of the biggest stars weren't making it until they had just a little work done."

John felt the hot fury of his anger break through. "But, Father dear, I look just like you, and you managed to score with Daisy!" Adam slammed his silverware down and stormed away from the table. John got up quietly and left.

As he drove away his thoughts were racing. He was sorry he had attacked Father, but he had long suspected that Daisy thought he needed a nose and ear job. He wondered if he really did look funny, but decided it was Daisy's "Hollywood" influence on Father. Nevertheless, his self-esteem was injured, and he began crying. He drove to a small club in Beverly Hills where he knew they'd serve him. He had three screwdrivers and felt pretty drunk. "How come you're not at Thad's party?" someone asked. John remembered Thad had told him to drop by.

Thad embraced John when he entered. John had never been there before and stood silently taking in the scene: psychedelic lights flashed on the walls, revealing posters of nude males. In the middle of the room couples of men were dancing, in a dark corner two men seemed engaged in sex play. Thad studied the blank look on John's face and correctly perceived his revulsion.

"Don't put it down, Johnny boy." John looked up as Thad continued, "We're all fags doing our thing, and you know what? You're one of us too! But you've been too uptight to come out. Well, why not now?" Thad leaned over and kissed him.

John stood there, paralyzed. Out of spite for Father he had an urge to join the party, and somewhere deep down he longed for the love of a man he remembered having as a little boy from Father. But he wasn't willing to renounce the strong masculine drives hidden under the passive defenses. He ran out of Thad's apartment, jumped in his car, and sped down the street toward Wilshire Boulevard. His foot was pressing with all his might on the accelerator as he crossed Wilshire against a red light. He swerved to miss a car, then a feeling of spinning through space, a terrible crashing noise, then silence.

The silent nothingness was still upon him when I first saw him. His mother had called me, and I had met with her and

John's father for a consultation. They explained that John had been in a terrible automobile accident, that he had crashed at high speed into the marble front of a building. He suffered a concussion and severe facial lacerations which had been sutured by an excellent plastic surgeon. He was being observed for internal injuries but it appeared he had escaped without anything more serious. The neurosurgeon felt that it was just a matter of time before he regained consciousness and that he had suffered no permanent brain damage.

The two of them seemed like old friends, and there was a minimum of uneasiness between them; their main concern was John. Father did most of the talking: "The police say he's damn lucky to be alive—must have been doing sixty! They think he was just another joy-riding drunk. We know differently—he wanted to kill himself."

Mother started sobbing, and when I looked to her she said, "Yes, that's true, we've checked a lot out since it happened." She was soft-spoken, gray, her hair pulled back in a knot. She was dressed nicely, but there was an old country look about her. Father was rather natty looking with his toupee and striking black moustache, but the newly wealthy businessman was no longer seeking youth and glamour. His old feelings of family devotion were strongly with him. I could see pain and guilt in his eyes.

Mother continued, "We know he had an argument with his father over plastic surgery on his nose, had a few drinks —he never ordinarily touches alcohol—then visited a homosexual friend . . ."

Father broke in, "That was Thad. God, I hate that queer! He was trying to get John to turn queer, I think, but as far as I know—please God!—he never was involved. Thad wouldn't tell us too much of what happened, but John got angry, ran out to his car, and a moment later, 'crash!' "

"He's been depressed really for several years," Mother continued, "since the divorce."

Father flinched but said nothing.

"I guess I tend to be depressed too, so I thought he just took after me. But I did worry about the friends he chose, and his father and I discussed that several times. We were thinking of suggesting he see a psychiatrist when this happened."

They went on to tell me about the changes they had noted during the past few years: his turning toward homosexual friends; his sullen, passive, provocative attitude toward his father; his preoccupation with the theatre and turning away from his old interest in law. They reproached themselves for not doing anything sooner. I agreed to see John in the hospital as soon as he was conscious.

On the third day of hospitalization the neurosurgeon called to tell me he had regained consciousness. I looked in on him that evening. As I approached he was sleeping. He was of medium size with a prominent nose and ears. There were signs of surgical repairs of several lacerations on his face. His eyes were swollen and purple. As I stood looking at him he opened his eyes and peered around the room. He saw me and said, "You the shrink?"

"Yes, I'm Dr. Wixen."

"Oh my God, do I need you!" He took my extended hand and held it with all his might as he began to sob. He clung to me for ten minutes or so, crying with deep shudders that shook his whole body. He seemed ashamed and kept his face turned toward the pillow. Finally the sobbing stopped and he released my hand.

"Shall we start work tomorrow?" I asked.

"Yes," he replied. "You'll see me while I'm here?"

I told him I'd see him the next day and left. When I arrived the next evening he was looking more alert and seemed happy to see me. We seemed to establish a good initial relationship, and he was genuinely eager for help. He described what had happened as best he could, although the hour before the accident was pretty fuzzy. He recalled feeling utter despair and not caring whether he lived or died.

He began analysis as soon as he left the hospital, a week later. He filled me in on the details of his early years and of his family. He was a bright and perceptive young man, mature beyond his years in some ways, and childlike in others. His passive-aggressive attitude toward his father quickly became the focus of our initial work. I was relieved to find that these traits were actually quite distasteful to him. For a long while there was no evidence of this pattern developing with me. We worked well together, and his deep hostility toward his father became more openly expressed. He realized the self-destructive methods he had used to express the deep hurt and resentment he felt. Gradually little hints of this same behavior began to appear toward me.

He started coming late for his appointments. At first there were more or less valid explanations, and then finally just a sullen shrug. This happens in analysis; the patterns of neurotic behavior that bring one into analysis begin being experienced toward the analyst. In the analytic situation the patient can experience the same patterns of behavior, while a part of himself stands aside and observes. There is thus a "split" into an experiencing portion and an observing portion. Where the earlier period of the analysis has established a firm basis of trust and understanding, the later stresses can be worked through. Few situations place greater strain on the analytic situation than the problem John had to reexperience and resolve.

His lateness became a regular occurrence and my interpretations to the effect that he was passively expressing hostility toward me did not change it. He came later and later, until he would sometimes arrive for only the last few minutes of his hour. He began speaking less and less until finally he spoke not at all. My various interpretations of his silence, and the obvious statement that the analysis could not proceed under these circumstances, were greeted with silence.

The *New Yorker* cartoons of analysts are usually amusing, but they fail to capture the analyst's *commitment* to his patient. Their analyst is looking at his watch, dozing, or revealing some idiosyncrasy of his own. Maybe it is frightening to think that there is a situation in this world where someone actually listens to every single utterance one makes and tries to understand it. Without question the analyst whose patient is in a silent angry state of negative transference suffers with his patient to an often painful degree. And yet he must retain his analytic position and his own equanimity. He has promised his patient that he will remain objective, that he will be as nonjudgmental as possible. The violation of this promise destroys the patient's trust and makes analysis impossible.

The image of the analyst as a blank screen only reflecting back the patient's associations is a schematic model to emphasize the analytic position he must maintain. Actually, while he observes and analyzes, and does his best to keep his own personal feelings from intruding, he is aware of these feelings and uses them to help him gain a fuller understanding of what is transpiring. During the hours of John's silence I could sympathize with his angry rage at me, I could understand the helpless desperation his father was driven to; I also had ample opportunity to reexperience my own needs to cure and to reflect on the danger of letting my frustration provoke me into any number of possible errors.

John never completely missed an appointment, and that seemed a hopeful indication of his involvement in the analysis; his silence was beyond his conscious control. "Hello, John," I said. He ignored me. He was five minutes late, looked depressed, and wearily reclined on the couch. I said, "John, you look depressed." Silence. After three or four minutes I tried again. "John, what is going through your mind?" Still no response. After a few more minutes (which seemed like an hour), "You must be terribly afraid of what you would say if you began speaking." He stared at the ceiling. A conference between me and me: "Should I withdraw and let him wait until he's ready? If I wait silently, will he interpret that as an angry, silent retaliation for what he is doing? If I keep prodding, will he feel I am picking on him? What in hell would Freud have done? What would Greenson do? How would Greenson and Freud have gotten along? I bet they would have competed for leadership—I'm wandering away from John. Should I tell him I feel like kicking him out? That would be devastating to him—but I feel like it. That must be what he wants me to feel!" And on and on.

Looking at him as he had come in, I could see depression

on his face. His shoulders were stooped, communicating his feeling of defeat. His eyes were bloodshot and his clothes disheveled. Everything about him told me he was suffering, and from the feelings he engendered in me, I was sure he wanted me to lose my temper and punish him. "John, you have been mostly silent for two weeks now. I am certain you feel miserable and depressed, and that you want me to get angry and scold or reject you." He was silent, and from his slow, steady breathing I realized he was asleep.

He slept for about ten minutes. He awoke with a start, sat up and looked around. He plopped back down. "What were you dreaming?" I asked. The dream reduced his anger enough so that he could speak.

"I was pissing on a snail. Snail—that's you."

"Me?"

"You know damn well what I mean—you have a shell around you that keeps you from getting hurt."

"Why were you pissing on me?"

"That's pretty clearly hostile, isn't it? Trying to get through your goddamn analytic armor to something human! Maybe if I flooded you with piss you'd come out for air."

"What else?" I asked.

"You want something more, huh? Not satisfied that I hate your bloody guts, your goddamn analytical defenses? What are you searching for? Pure hatred isn't enough for you? You are an arrogant, conceited, self-centered, inhuman, rigid, cold son of a bitch! There's only one thing I can't understand."

"What's that?"

"How can you put up with me?" And with that John began crying uncontrollably.

JOHN

The crying continued for the rest of the hour. He had gained insight into the passive-aggressive mechanisms he used with his father, he had reexperienced them with me in the analysis. He had broken through them to the underlying anger at Father, and just below that anger was his self-hate and his longing to be loved.

The analysis lasted four years. His father's leaving him and Mother had provoked a great deal of anger. More deeply hidden was the self-hate. Children often interpret family disasters as a result of some misdeed on their part and hate themselves for it. John had adopted a passive-submissive attitude toward his father, but under that was a guilt-filled rivalry. At the time of the divorce John thought—in the self-centered way children often do—"Dad is leaving because Mother and I are so *plain,* because I'm such an ugly blah, because I disappoint him so much." He would spend hours in front of a mirror hating and cursing his nose and ears (since he also looked very much like his father, he was also venting his anger at him, but that part was largely unconscious). This helps explain why the comments about his nose and ears on the night of the accident had such a violent effect on him.

There were other things to uncover and resolve: his flirtation with homosexuality, his deep love for his mother lying under his attachment to Father, his conflict about competing with men. After our one major crisis in his analysis the work proceeded fairly smoothly. He returned to college, and we terminated the analysis just before he entered law school.

Clearly, the problem posed by John is much closer to the neurotic problems ordinarily encountered by psychiatrists. But there were special problems added by the rapid upward change in social status. John had been imbued with middle-class values during the formative years of his childhood: "Work, study, get ahead, make something of yourself, look what Grampa's children accomplished, look at your uncles—one's a judge and one's dean of a medical school, practice your violin." While this was a heavy load to saddle a child with, John was quite capable of handling the load.

What went wrong here was the sudden mixing of middle-class values for achievement with a whole new style of living that made them seem unnecessary and irrelevant. "I am supposed to work and create something while my father chases after youth and screws around in Las Vegas?" The old identifications no longer were sources of gratification; his early identification with his father was disrupted by the changes that occurred in him.

If John's family had not become suddenly wealthy, he still might someday have sought analysis to resolve conflicts concerning assertiveness and sexuality. But his situation was tremendously compounded by the upward mobility. This almost proved fatal for John. Less dramatic cases of a similar nature are frequently encountered.

There are other possible outcomes of the emotional stresses that may follow rapid upward mobility. Unlike the dysgradia of the CORs, the problems of mobility neuroses are manifested more clearly in terms of emotional suffering rather than a particular type of empty life-style. Some of those who are caught in the identity crises of upward mobility successfully avoid suffering by adopting new life-styles. These may be "healthy" or "sick" depending on the particular situation and the bias of the observer.

26

NEW LIFE-STYLES

RAPID UPWARD MOBILITY ALMOST INVARIABLY PRODUCES identity crises; these may lead to various different outcomes. One interesting occurrence at the present time involves an apparent resolution by means of adopting an entirely new life-style. A common example is the affluent dropout. No final evaluation of this trend is yet possible, but it deserves intensive study.

A typical situation: Matt, an only child, has grown up in Brentwood and led "the good life." His father worked his way from a real estate salesman to president of a large investment firm. When Matt is sixteen his parents rather suddenly become alarmed by his late hours and poor grades. A series of serious fights, interspersed with chronic tension, persists between him and his parents for the next year. Drugs are added to the caldron and there are a number of LSD trips and regular use of marijuana. There is one attempt at psychotherapy, but Matt refuses to continue after meeting with me once.

By his seventeenth birthday he has dropped out of high school and stays in his room all day. He goes out every night or has friends over to smoke grass and listen to music. His family tries everything—pleading, threats, bribery—but feels completely defeated. Matt warns them to quit bugging him or he will leave home. They don't and he does.

Matt is not heard from for the next year and a half. A private detective engaged by the family locates him on a commune in New Mexico. He now has a full beard, a black wife given to Hindu readings, and an infant daughter.

"Come home?" A long, not forced laugh. "I am home. My wife and family are here."

His mother is crying, "Oh Matt, I don't know where we failed but we're sorry! Please, please! Bring your wife and baby and come back with us."

"Why?"

"Why?—Because this shack isn't fit to live in. You have no toilets, the place must leak like a shower in the rain. There are no schools—and everyone here looks high on dope."

"Some of them are. Each of us here is free to live as he sees fit. Man survived for eons without marble toilets. We have our own school where we teach the children what we feel is important, in our own way. We teach the importance of the earth and of love. We do without color television—or radio for that matter—and we grow our own healthy food. Your smog-filled, insecticide-polluted city isn't fit to live in."

The discussion goes on for several hours but ends up with the same impasse. Matt refuses to accept any money from them and refuses to promise to write. "I can't write you. The post office in town is twenty miles away and we have no cars. The sheriff hassles us when we come to town, so we stay away. And anyway, we have nothing to say to each other."

"But you're our son—we're your parents. We love you . . ." Mother and Father try desperately to make contact, but there is none. They leave heartbroken.

I can't tell you in detail what motivated Matt to adopt this new life-style. I saw him once when he was seventeen. He was very bright and well read. He had an almost analytical detachment from his parents whose life-style he discussed freely and critically.

"They are having fits because I don't want to go into Dad's business. I've had it with school because it's all Establishment brainwashing. I have a list of great books of the world—and not just the white man's world. I study them in my room or at the library. The East has much to teach us. So do those outside the Establishment."

I tried to probe for areas of conflict.

He understood and answered, "I went through the spoiled brat scene. Then something happened. My parents started hassling me. I met some really wise friends and started reading a lot. Then they started hassling me even more. If you're a spoiled brat you get hassled and if you become concerned with the rest of the world you get hassled."

"You seem angry with your parents," I said.

"You're damn right I am. But lately I've begun to feel sorry for them, too. They're so caught up in the country club business. And making money. And making more money. That means nothing to me. If they don't stop hassling me, I'll split." He showed some anger at them, but there was also a touch of pity.

I made no effort to debate the value of his family's way of life with him, nor the accuracy of his view of it. I did urge him to come back to talk more about his feelings, and he said simply, "No."

Matt seemed to have gone through a more or less typical identity crisis seen in the children of families who have made major jumps in social position. Instead of resolving it after a period of turbulence—often admixed with the more usual features of adolescent rebellion—as is the most usual outcome, he took a different path. He did not become neurotic; there were no symptoms, no depression, only an increasing alienation from his family. Finally he made a complete break and adopted a radically new life-style.

I can tell you more about the family background from another source: his mother came to me for a few visits after her trip to New Mexico. She was suffering from a moderate depression. The therapy amounted to helping her through a period of mourning; for her, her son was dead.

One facet from the parents' background may have some bearing on the direction Matt's identity crisis resolution took.

NEW LIFE-STYLES

They had both been "revolutionaries" in college. After their disenchantment with Communism, they actively supported liberal causes, especially civil rights. At the same time, they had servants and were actively seeking status. I detected more than a touch of disgust with their less liberal neighbors and on the wife's part a touch of guilt about her own wealth.

Much of Matt's new life-style was built upon a reversal, a negative identification with his parents. But was there something more than a new identity built upon repudiating the old? Did he in some way identify with his parents' old revolutionary zeal? Did their old idealism somehow get transmitted to him and blossom to a fruition they never dared dream of? Did the parents unconsciously sanction and encourage his dropping out? Did they vicariously fulfill their frustrated idealism at his expense? There are no answers to these questions—only a history of a past idealism lost in their new materialism.

A few more points must be explored. Was Matt's new life a neurotic acting-out? Not by the usual criteria. Was it a bold new break with the past, a triumph of idealism—or a regressive step backward, a cowardly retreat from the demands of the real world? The answer given must depend on one's bias. One can ask the question: Is this behavior adaptive? But again there is no objective answer. Matt was capable of considerable achievement in the middle-class milieu, but he was a respected leader and teacher in his commune.

I feel there is a waste here, a tragedy. But I recognize that Matt could answer all the arguments one could muster, and there is no evidence of neurotic suffering. Time will tell; my guess is he'll come back.

27

CONCLUSION

LOS ANGELES HAS CHANGED A GREAT DEAL FROM THOSE clear blue days I remember in the thirties. When the mountains to the north are visible after a cleansing rainstorm, the newspapers will feature a photo on the front page for those who missed the view. The changes in the social vistas during these years have also been dramatic.

Huge numbers of people have accumulated great sums of

CONCLUSION

wealth; the corresponding shifts in their social status have been tremendous. Values, ideals, role images—the components of one's sense of identity—have met with changes in a few decades that are greater than the changes of preceding centuries. It is perhaps remarkable that so many people have adjusted to the new realities. Social scientists are only beginning to know very much about man's capacity to adapt to such rapid changes. Historically, nothing comparable has ever happened.

Among those who fail to make the necessary adaptations to these changes, a variety of problems may develop. I have drawn attention to a particular type of problem, seen quite often among the very wealthy, which I have termed dysgradia. In this situation there is a breakdown in the passage of necessary ideas concerning meaningful self-images from one generation to the next. The result is a deficiency in the individual's capacity to derive gratification from his efforts and thereby maintain his self-esteem. A life of wasted wealth and energy may be the outcome of the desperate efforts to escape the feelings of emptiness.

It appears that man will be able to cope with the rapid social and technological changes well enough to assure his physical survival. But we are concerned with more than physical survival: can man make the necessary psychological adjustments to provide a state of emotional equilibrium? What kind of future does a species have in which its members are assured of basic survival, but are overwhelmed by the rapidity of change and reduced to a state of chronic confusion and despair? We do not know; perhaps we should not underestimate man's capacity for psychological adaptation. While such global questions are of increasing concern to psychiatrists, the basic focus remains on helping the individual.

The fragrant orange groves just outside Los Angeles have been replaced with lovely (and not so lovely) new communities. Huge numbers of upper-middle-class homes are occupied by people whose families were solidly poor and lower-middle-class not too many years ago. The lower-middle-class neighborhood I grew up in is now deep in an immense black ghetto. The new rich and the trapped poor are both confronted with problems brought about by conflicts between their psychological heritage and the world they find themselves in. The poor must adapt a heritage of passive and obedient roles to an aggressive, competitive society. The new rich must reconcile obsolete values and ideals to a new world of affluence. The young people are the casualties of these identity problems.

A disturbed child from the black ghetto cannot be treated with the same psychotherapeutic techniques that would be effective for an upper-middle-class child. Neither can an upper-class youth suffering from dysgradia. This book has been about the types of problems encountered and the therapeutic means of helping the very wealthy patient and those involved in rapid upward movement in their socioeconomic status.

That the very poor are much more numerous, and their problems much more urgent at this time, is indisputable. Focusing on the other end of the spectrum is intended to fill in some empty spaces in our thinking rather than to suggest a shift in priorities. Wherever human potential is being wasted, wherever human suffering is not dealt with, thoughtful people must be concerned.

CONCLUSION

There has never been a classless society, though there are societies in which power rather than wealth draws the distinctions. And there are societies in which massive poverty or tyranny makes social mobility almost unthinkable. Hopefully, America will continue to be concerned with assisting its people in becoming upwardly mobile, and the behavioral scientists will continue to be concerned with the problems that result.

Overpopulation and exhaustion of our natural resources could reverse that trend. If that should occur, the behavioral scientists of the future will look back on this book as an amusing historical curiosity. Perhaps someday volumes will be written on the social problems of an overextended society in which huge numbers of people are reduced from a life of affluence to one of survival.

Some feel it is already too late. Some aren't aware enough of the dangers to be frightened. Without awareness and without hope no change is possible. To be torn between hope and despair is to face reality.